HABEAS BRITANNIAM

British Liberty & The Legal Case against the EU

Dominic Bardill

ISBN:1530969565
ISBN-13:9781530969562

DEDICATION

To Her Majesty Elizabeth the Second, by the Grace of God of the United Kingdom of Great Britain and Northern Ireland, and of Her other Realms and Territories Queen, Head of the Commonwealth, Defender of the Faith, in her 90th year of life and her 64th year of reign; and to a strong, free and independent United Kingdom.

CONTENTS

ACKNOWLEDGMENTS

SPECIAL THANKS TO
Timothé Buffet; Diana Bardill; Jamie Ross McKenzie; Nathan Somerville, Thomas Turton & Richard McCarthy.

COVER DESIGNED & CREATED BY
Jamie Ross McKenzie.

PREFACE

During my studies of English Law, it became quickly apparent to me that the people of the United Kingdom has developed and inherited the most wonderful claim: The claim to have invented, amongst many other things, a true concept of liberty. As my studies moved further along, into the abyss of European Union Law, it quickly became clear to me that The European Union had become so engrained into the smallest details of our lives and existence, that our own allegiances had become misplaced. People would talk often about the Human Rights Act, as if it were a founding principle of liberty, seemingly ignorant of the Charter of Liberties, or the Magna Carta. All of the positive aspects of our lives were being made to appear 'European' (in the false, manufactured EU sense of the word), whilst the true foundations of liberty were being long forgotten.

This I considered to be the reason why so many people were allowing the great inheritance manifest in our laws and liberties, to be forgotten and replaced, by inferior versions. This was the inspiration, and motivation, for this *Habeas Britanniam*. The title, translates [very] roughly to 'May you have Britain'. To me, this expression sums up the mentality of those who passed on the greatest legal system, and with it the unique freedoms that come with being British or living in the United Kingdom. I wanted to convey the truth of our liberties, past and present, to the average person. We often here of the economic, or socio-political arguments against the European Union, however, to me, all of these subjects ultimately fall under the law, and the law ultimately relates to liberty. Consequently, I wrote this book as someone who is impassioned by the United Kingdom's constitution and common law system. I am proud of the United Kingdom's legal achievements and I believe it is the ultimate liberty of every individual, to know what their liberties actually are and how the EU threatens them. Indeed EU law is a notoriously difficult, vast and complex area, so using sources like journals, articles, newspapers, case law, statute, EU laws, commentaries, and books, I have tried to reduce them to the relevant areas concerning the individual.

This book is not exhaustive, but I hope your reading of it may provoke some critical thought, and equip you with knowledge and arguments that you can use in your daily lives. During my studies of English and European Union law, my eyes were opened. During the long process, of researching and writing this book, my eyes were opened even more. I hope, that during your reading of this book, the complicated and vast subject of EU law will become clear and understandable. I hope that your eyes may be opened to what you have, what you may lose and what you can gain in life, for yourself and for your country. You will often find, that the two are deeply intertwined. I hope, that after reading this, you will understand what I mean when I say 'May you have Britain', or '*Habeas Britannia!*'

Habeas Britanniam

CHAPTER 1
THE SOURCES OF ENGLISH LAW

There are two sources of Law in England and Wales, one is the common law; law that emanates from and is developed by the courts as a result of decided cases, legal principles and judicial reasoning. The other source is Statute –those codified laws that come from Parliament; otherwise known as 'acts of Parliament'.

Common law is the legal system of choice in various nations across the globe. In particular, aside from the United Kingdom, you will find that it is in use across the Commonwealth and in the United States of America. The underlying foundation of common law is the legal principle *'stare decisis'* which translated into English means 'let the decision stand'. Essentially, this principle underpins the common law system by binding decisions that are made by judges, onto all other judges. The practical result of this is a legal system that has the flexibility to approach new situations, cases or circumstances quickly, whilst being guided by a set of continuously developing principles. Principles that are based on previous decisions made in similar cases, over a long period of time. This means that in common law, all people really are equal before the law, since *stare decisis* means that two decisions that are made on similar facts must have similar outcomes. In other words, if two people commit the same crime, in the same circumstances, then they will receive the same punishment regardless of who the judge is. This is known as the doctrine of precedent, and it is one of the most important yet simple principles, that make our law courts far more accountable and fair than the vast majority of others on the planet.

The beauty of this precedent is that the law itself, though developed by judges either making rulings or interpreting statute, is still nonetheless transcended by the common law. All rulings are usually binding on subordinate judges and courts, equal judges and courts, and future judges and courts. In England and Wales, we have several courts for both criminal and civil (or non-criminal) matters. There is a hierarchy amongst these courts; the lowest being the Magistrates Court; then the Crown Court; then the High Court, then the Court of Appeal and finally the Supreme Court (formerly the House of Lords). Generally cases will progress through the courts, depending on whether a judge refers cases or outcomes are appealed, and each court is able to overrule the court below. This means that the Supreme Court can overrule judgments on all other courts and bind them via the doctrine of precedent, making it the highest court in the land, which only Parliament, using Parliamentary Sovereignty, can overrule by using Acts of Parliament. There are issues however, with the introduction of European Courts into the English legal system, which you will notice when you come across some examples as we go along.

The opposite of common law, and I use the term opposite

because in my view all of the virtues of common law are ultimately subverted within this system, is Civil Law. Civil Law acts on the idea of codified law that works from the top down. Essentially, it looks, as we will explore later, at the 'letter of the law' rather than the intention behind it, which means that the doctrine of precedent that is so central to common law and provides continuity and consistency, is absent. In a Civil Law jurisdiction, such as France, Germany or most of the European Countries, a previous judge's ruling is not binding on subsequent judges, but is merely 'persuasive'.

Statute law, as I mentioned previously, comes about by Act of Parliament. Parliament enacts the law by passing a motion through both houses and if both houses pass it then the legislation becomes law —except for certain circumstances. An Act of Parliament is ultimately the highest form of law in the United Kingdom because of the important constitutional principle of Parliamentary Sovereignty. Accordingly, the only way a decision that is binding on courts through common law can be overturned is if Parliament legislates to do so. So for example, Common Assault was an offence in common law that was defined in the case of *Fagan v Metropolitan Police Commissioner* as when an individual; *"...intentionally or recklessly causes the victim to apprehend immediate unlawful personal violence[1]."* This offence, through the common law system mentioned above, was brought about and developed by the judicial system, with various definitions used to interpret or give context to the words therein, found in other cases. However in 1988 the Criminal Justice Act was passed which codified common law assault; thus turning it into a

---

[1] *Fagan v. Metropolitan Police Commissioner* [1968] 1 QB 439

statutory offence by virtue of section 39 of said act which states;

> *"Common assault and battery shall be summary offences and a person guilty of either of them shall be liable to a fine not exceeding level 5 on the standard scale, to imprisonment for a term not exceeding six months, or to both[2]."*

Upon making it a statutory offence, any conflict with the existing case law or precedents would render the case law or precedent null and void; statute always takes priority over common law. Interestingly, the Statute does not actually provide the definition within it of 'Common Assault'. So the original common law definition is still referred to for the definition of this crime, however the principle I wish to highlight here is the hierarchy of the law in a common law system, with regards to Acts of Parliament. Thus, if Parliament had decided to say that the definition would be such that a weapon must be used in order for it to be an assault, then the previous definition would no longer stand, and the new statutory definition would come into play.

As already pointed out, in this instance, the original common law definition is still referred to as the source of the definition of common law, whilst the offence itself is codified into a statutory offence by virtue of the Act of Parliament. This is another reason why I decided to use common assault as an example; not only does it highlight how common law develops, defines and even creates law, as well as how statute has authority over common law, but it also shows their unique and pragmatic interaction. Common law frequently provides definition, or context, to

---

[2] Criminal Justice Act 1988, c.33, Part v, S. 39

statute. Sometimes -indeed quite often, statute can be worded in such a way as to cause confusion, be unclear or at the very least be very impractical in applying to real life situations. Consequently, judges have various tools and rules of interpretation, that allow them to refer to case law or use reasoning to provide practical and useful definitions to words contained within the statute. In the illustration of common assault, we see that Parliament saw it fit to codify the offence, they were themselves content with the original definition, and this shows perfectly how common law allows immediate questions of law that arise in the real world to be addressed, meaning that Parliament can focus on legislating for larger, on-going or pressing matters of law. Contrast this with a Civil Code, and you will see that the absence of real judicial authority to develop law, essentially an absence of the common law system, means that the respective Parliament must spend uncountable hours debating, codifying and legislating on trivial matters. In short, civil law is impractical because it cannot keep up with the social environment, nor is it useful to expect a Parliament to imagine every conceivable situation and legislate accordingly.

These reasons and many others are why the common law system which compliments a legislature, is so incredibly superior and works so well by comparison. It is for this reason that the UK Constitution has continuously proven to be superior and advanced to this day, despite tracing back its roots centuries ago. The United Kingdom's constitution was born out of the common law system, and so it too carries with it the advantages, practicalities, pragmatism and pure astuteness that are inherent in the common law system. It is important therefore to have an understanding of how common law has formed the United

Kingdom's constitutional setup, because in understanding this we can better understand how the common law system benefits you personally, even today in the 21st century, as an individual with all your liberties and freedoms. I think it is a good idea then, to explore the roots of the common law system, and how this developed into the constitution that has invisibly watched over us for centuries and generations.

CHAPTER 2
THE CHARTER OF LIBERTIES

In exploring where the United Kingdom got its common law system, and the principles that underpin the constitution itself, it is wise to look first at the original idea of liberty in what was then England. Many people incorrectly assume the Magna Carta to be the root of the United Kingdom's Constitution and liberty itself. Undeniably it is perhaps one of the most important aspects of liberty, but it cannot be said to be the fountain from which liberty sprung. Indeed, the real forbearer of liberty came over a century earlier in the year 1100 with King Henry I, upon his becoming King. This is why it is often known as the Coronation Charter.

Unlike many monarchs before and after him, King Henry I was exceptionally well educated and cultured[3]. This formidable upbringing, at least by the standards of that period, provided Henry with the ability to read and write in the Latin language. Ultimately, his linguistic and scholastic ability meant that he was well placed to become an expert

---

[3] Hollister, C. Warren (2003). Frost, Amanda Clark, ed. p. 36 – 37, *Henry I*. New Haven, US and London, UK: Yale University Press.

in possibly the most important tool that any nation possesses: the law. Henry's knowledge of English law meant that Henry had a particularly unique outlook on the administration of his Kingdom. Furthermore, his father, William the Conqueror, may have also influenced Henry heavily, as the story goes. One may even go so far as to say that Henry's love of English law may have sprung from his Father's death.

The claim is that the very first Charter of Liberties actually came from William the Conqueror when he became convinced that his last days were approaching him, due to ill health. William is said to have written a Charter, which contained unprecedented actions; from absolving debts, pardoning criminals, handing out money to the Church and individuals, and releasing prisoners. The reality is however, that we don't truly know what William intended to do with the Charter because the only copy was destroyed, and the words were never recorded or passed on for generations to see and enjoy. Consequently, whilst it can be claimed that the original Charter of Liberties came from William the Conqueror, it can only sustainably be claimed that his son Henry I provided the first Charter that would be implemented into English law. Nonetheless, the argument could still be made that this Charter may well have been inspired by, and an ancestor of, the pending actions in William's.

Henry I was not exactly a popular King when he came to claim the throne of England. The Church at the time behaved in a very stubborn and provocative way, whilst the Barons of England refused to recognise him, as did the Anglo-Saxon subjects. All three of these elements were of absolutely vital importance to any prospective English

King, and necessary if one was to rule in an efficient manner. Henry's knowledge of English law meant that he knew this; he also knew how to solve the problem too. Thus came the Charter of Liberties 1100, which came into effect on Henry I's Coronation.

What does this ancient document mean to us today in the modern world? Well the answer is that is all depends! It depends on what we value as a society, what we know about our own heritage and history, and what we understand to be necessary in order to accomplish true freedom for any individual. The problem today however, is that the concept of the individual has gone from being a term of autonomy, to instead being a term of selfishness. In Britain, many people still have a very British mind-set about individual rights and freedoms, yet at the same time are often influenced by a more continental approach to upholding and enforcing these ideas. The inevitable and evident result of this is that the mixture of increasing continental methods, with the undying British mind-set, creates a series of absurdities.

There is a hugely significant element to this Charter, which is worth noting in the current war of ideology being waged between Eurosceptics and Europhiles across Europe and more specifically here in the United Kingdom. That element, which draws from it an enormous relevance to our own situation several centuries on, relates to Henry I's motivation in professing the Charter. In the face of potential rebellion or non-compliance from his Bishops, Barons and Subjects, Henry I sought to create confidence in him that the English were not to be ruled by a foreign method. Indeed, for the Anglo-Saxon subjects in particular, the idea of a King from Normandy ruling over their land created an unease of vast proportions[4] and his claim to the English throne ultimately sat on a knife-edge.

This is one of the reasons why Henry I's coronation was so rushed, but it is also one of the many reasons why Henry I devised his Charter of Liberties. Bishop Stubbs claimed that the Charter was an amplification of the coronation oath, and that it was a rejection of the foreign, evil ways, as much as it was an express devotion to the ways of England. Stubbs claimed, that the underlying principle of this, was a principle based on a yearning that the Anglo-Saxons had, and one that could be argued is still appropriate in todays climate; a return to 'national government':

> *"...it is a recognition of the lawful freedom of the nation, which those evil customs had infringed, and which was regarded as symbolised by the laws of Edward the Confessor. Further, it is an exemplification of the evil customs themselves; and historically marks the amount of departure from free and national government which had prevailed in the late reign[5]."*

The contents of the Charter are of course rather important if one is to understand what kinds of liberties were being bestowed on the land from the King. The Charter, in essence, concerned mainly the nobility and barons; addressing concerns they had about the tyranny of the monarchs that had gone before Henry I. Naturally then, one might assume it holds little relevance to ordinary people and is thus insignificant with regards to the ordinary rights and liberties that are enjoyed today. This could not be further from the truth however, and in due course it

---

[4] J. M. Lappenberg, *History of England Under the Angevin Kings*, Vol. 1 (1887)
[5] Stubbs, William. (2013). pp. 98-9. *Select Charters and Other Illustrations of English Constitutional History*. London: Forgotten Books. (Original work published 1905)

shall become clear why.

The words, in English, of the Charter of Liberties 1100 were as follows:

> "I, Henry, by the grace of God having been crowned the King of England, shall not take or sell any property from a Church upon the death of a bishop or abbot, until a successor has been named to that Church property. I shall end all the oppressive practices that have been an evil presence in England.
>
> 2.) If any baron or earl of mine shall die, his heirs shall not be forced to purchase their inheritance, but shall retrieve it through force of law and custom.
>
> 3.) Any baron or earl who wishes to betroth his daughter or other women kinsfolk in marriage should consult me first, but I will not stand in the way of any prudent marriage. Any widow who wishes to remarry should consult with me, but I shall abide by the wishes of her close relatives, the other barons and earls. I will not allow her to marry one of my enemies.
>
> 4.) Any wife of my barons, who becomes a widow shall not be denied her dowry. She should be allowed to remarry according to her wishes, so long as she maintains the integrity of her body, in a lawful manner. Barons overseeing the children of a dead baron shall maintain their land and interest in a lawful manner.
>
> 5.) Common seigniorages taken in the cities and counties, which was not taken in the time of Edward I (Edward the Confessor), shall henceforth be forbidden.
>
> 6.) I shall remit [cancel] all debts and pleas which were owing to my brother, except those which were lawfully made through an inheritance.

7.) If any of my barons should grow feeble, and give away money or other possessions, these shall be honored, so long as the heirs are properly remembered. Gifts given by feeble barons under force of arms shall not be enforced.

8.) If any of my barons commit a crime, he shall not bind himself to the crown with a payment as was done in the time of my father and brother, but shall stand for the crime as was custom and law before the time of my father, and make amends as are appropriate. Anyone guilty of treachery or other heinous crime shall make proper amends.

9.) I forgive all murders committed before I was crowned. Subsequent murders shall stand before the justice of the Crown.

10.) With the common consent of my barons, I shall maintain all the forests as was done in the time of my father.

11.) Those knights who render military service and horses shall not be required to give grain or other farm goods to me.

12.) I impose a strict peace on the land, and command it be maintained.

13.) I restore the law of King Edward and the amendments which my father introduced upon the advice of his barons.

14.) Anything taken from me after the death of my father shall be returned immediately, without fine. If it is not returned, a heavy fine shall be enforced.

Witnesses Maurice bishop of London, and William bishop elect of Winchester, and Gerard bishop of Hereford, and earl Henry, and earl Simon, and Walter Giffard, and Robert de Montfort, and Roger Bigot, and Eudo the steward, and Robert son of Hamo, and Robert Malet. At London when I was crowned. Farewell[6]."

It can plainly be seen then, that the Charter of Liberties brought into force immeasurably unique concepts, well ahead of their time. Ultimately, Henry I bestowed great benevolence over the people of his Kingdom. He absolved debts, pushed forward the right to inherit or leave an estate, to marry as one saw fit (to a point), dealt with corruption in the church such as simony (selling sacraments), and even led the way in terms of issues that might today be described as 'women's rights'. Certainly by todays standards women still did not enjoy a freedom that the modern world might say is a right, but there is no denying that because the Charter was the first of its kind, Henry I was leading the way by giving women in England greater rights in inheritance, family and marriage.

Indeed his allowances to people in general extended much further than the Kingdoms across the continent could even contemplate. Henry I, essentially brought into force, all or most of the rights, freedoms and liberties, that his father is said to have wanted to bequeath to the nation, and perhaps in some ways even more. The most significant of all however, is that Henry I restored a principle that in the United Kingdom today has long been held to be of so much importance, that it is regarded as a constitutional convention. That is, the 'rule of law'.

Henry I specifically mentions, in a number of the sections above, that the law that is to rule, equally over all men, was to be the law of Edward the Confessor. Why is this so significant? Well, aside from the fact that Edward the Confessor was a King of huge popularity, and one whose

---

[6] Charter of Liberties, 1100 A.D. (National Humanities Institute) - http://www.nhinet.org/ccs/docs/char-lib.htm

reign was highly regarded; he was also the last of the Anglo-Saxon, or English, Kings. The significance of this, cuts to the heart of the issue mentioned by Bishop Stubbs; the King was restoring national government, under national laws, and by national means. King Henry I gave England the right to rule herself, and he did so by wiping clean the slate that had been smeared and chipped by some of his Norman predecessors and taking England back to her roots. At the same time as taking England back, Henry also brought England forward way ahead of any other nation. How interesting that England at the time of Edward the Confessor, had a better system than the England that Henry I inherited, and than the countries across the seas! Henry saw the value and necessity in national government, and specifically in the unique and innovative way that England had governed herself in the past, which set a sterling example to the world by the standards of the day. Whilst the Charter was not itself law, it contained promises that enshrined the idea of self-governance, because he recognised the power in autonomy and the danger in tyranny. Additionally however, it enshrined this idea by enshrining the idea of self-governance for the individual, which is what made the whole Charter so uniquely British and so fantastically libertarian. Each person shall govern himself just as the country governs herself, the Kingdom was to be run on the principle of autonomy and sovereignty.

Evidence of the fact that this spread down to the individual can be seen in the wording of the Charter which addresses a series of issues relating to individual rights in addition to restoring the law of Edward the Confessor. However, it is also evident in its results, which like a healthy, prosperous tree, sprung sweet and plentiful fruits for the subjects of the land; at least for a while. Sir Jonathan Frederick Pollock; a 1st Baronet, Member of Parliament and notable lawyer, during the 1800s, regarded Henry I's Charter as being of huge importance to the constitutional makeup of the country, as well as to the legal field in general. In his book; 'The History of English Law before the Time of Edward I', he deals with it at great length. He notes that Henry I's expectation of the Barons and nobles that were to benefit from the promises made in the Charter was that they would do the same for their tenants. This is ultimately how it affected ordinary people, because for the first time in English history, the general public were to benefit from the same rights, as individuals, as the nobles. Indeed, it is likely that this would have taken place to some extent, for example as those providing military assistance were taxed less, so too were the tenants.

However, the glory of this Charter did not shine as brightly as the Charter, or the King, had implied that it would. Pollock disputes whether the Charter itself really had any practical effect. In particular, Pollock makes the point that Henry himself, failed to observe the Charter, saying;

> "...we can hardly treat this charter as an act of legislation. It is rather a promise that the law disregarded by Rufus shall henceforth be observed. This promise in after times became a valuable precedent, but it could not be enforced against the king, and Henry did not observe it [7]."

The point remains however, that this Charter, whether the practical effect was a desired one or not, gives a great insight into the values and liberties that the people of England demanded. Upon examination of the text, and the

---

[7] Pollock, Frederick; Maitland, William (1968) [1898]. p. 95, *History of English Law before the time of Edward I*. Cambridge University Press.

underlying principles, you will see that in relation to foreign jurisdictions, these freedoms and liberties were exceptionally advanced in conceptual terms for that period. If there is any legal document that demonstrates the formidable aptitude of what would just a few centuries later become the United Kingdom, for encompassing and recognising the true natural liberties of man, then it is this. It may have had little practical effect, since it was introduced at a time when other conventions, customs and values were not in place to check and balance it; the foundations were laid nonetheless, for what was to follow.

CHAPTER 3
THE ASSIZE OF CLARENDON

Imagine for a moment, that a corpse has been found lying in a ditch. The body is of someone known to you, and with whom you did not have the best relations, and this is no secret to the mutual friends and acquaintances that you both keep. The police, naturally, are investigating, and they become convinced, despite little concrete evidence besides testimonies from your mutual associates, that it was you who bludgeoned this individual to death, and they soon arrive on your doorstep.

"You're under arrest for murder!" The words pierce through you like the sharpest of knives. You cannot quite believe what you have heard, but you have no time to think as the handcuffs are clasped around your wrists and you are thrown into a cold, damp, menacing cell. Hours pass –they soon become days. You sit in the cell, with no windows or doors and no knowledge of how much time has passed.

Suddenly, a bright light stings your eyes as the cell door opens. You blink harshly, and before you can fully regain your vision you are pulled from the cell and march before a judge, who proceeds to convict you on his own judgment without a shred of evidence and sentence you to death.

No fair trial, no conviction on the basis of evidence, no chance to retort against the claims made about you; ultimately, no justice. One would be hard pressed to find a decent, civilised human being who did not consider that scenario to be particularly horrific. Nevertheless, if your home had been the 10th Century, in any nation on the European Continent, then that may well have been your bitter end, as it was the bitter fate of many thousands of other potentially innocent people.

In 1166, King Henry II of England was charged with the task of overseeing an arguably unstable and tense Kingdom. At the time of his reign, the Crusades were well underway, which caused copious amounts of difficulties in relation to the administration of justice and law throughout his Kingdom. English law did not make many provisions concerning land; despite land having always been an immensely valuable commodity in England –which remains the case today. Due to the wars being waged against the rise of Islam in the Byzantine East, many noble men went away to fight, leaving people to occupy their land; people who would come to be known as 'squatters'. When a soldier died in battle, the English legal system was incapable of dividing his estate, or working out what was even a part of his estate and what was not.

Aside from squatters and disputes over land ownership, the law also faced issues with the Church. King Henry did not like the fact that the Church had its own legal system and courts. He believed that there should be only one law, under the crown, and all must be subject to it. The reality was that the Church was incredibly asset rich, one of the principal assets being land. This vast wealth and land-ownership, coupled with the independent judicial system, meant that the Church exercised enormous societal influence in a political arena that King Henry believed far exceeded that which it rightfully had jurisdiction over. Moreover, the Church with its cast land wealth and independent legal system, were answerable to the Pope rather than the King; thus, Henry viewed this as the Church being *'imperium in imperio'*, essentially a Kingdom within a Kingdom. To the King, this was unacceptable not due to personal egotistical covetous desires for more land and money (such as was the case with Henry VIII), nor a pride and vanity. It was unacceptable because it created an inequality in the law between different members of society, and created a means by which members of the clergy and Church nobility, could escape the accountability that other subjects could not. It essentially made the law unworkable, and inept.

There was also an enormous issue with criminality. The significant increase in criminal acts had been the result of unpaid mercenaries and those who had lost possessions and livelihoods in recent civil wars. This meant that those in poverty, or those who were vengeful and yet skilled, would profit from criminal and sometimes violent acts; the King realised that this could not be permitted in any stable nation, and sought to put a stop to it.

The Assize of Clarendon represented the start of what would become the foundations of English Common Law. It cemented into the English legal system, two things; first, the unification of Law in England. For too long various wealthy land owners and Barons exercised immense power due to essentially having their own laws. This resulted in different laws, in different areas of the country, which gave rise to discrepancies and ambiguities as to what the law in a given geographical area was. The King, through the Assize of Clarendon, was exercising an equitable judgment based on an idea well ahead of its time; he believed that everyone who is expected to obey the law, has a what could be described as an equitable right to know what that law is. The only way this was achievable was by removing the jurisdiction from the hands of the Barons, and unifying the courts under the crown as one English Law, exercisable in a unified set of courts.

The second element was that of the creation of what was to become the 'Grand Jury', and the right to be tried by Jury. The King appointed a series of Judges, who, instead of staying with one geographical area administering the law under the Baron there, would instead draw their authority from the Crown and travel throughout the land. The idea was that each Judge's decision would bind other Judges, and the same principles and law would guide them all. These Judges would arrive in the jurisdiction, and 15 freemen would be chosen. This concept of trial by Jury, as well as the system being the first ever system to perform trial by evidence, far exceeded the innovation of our European Counterparts who were still practising trial by duel, or trial by inquisition. This demonstrates what can only be described, albeit admittedly with an air of arrogance, a sense of superiority in the English legal system pre-dating the European Union by some centuries. It represented the beginning of the end of a feudal system where the power lay in the hands of Barons and brought such powers under the Royal Courts and the judiciary, which provided a more equitable foundation. It meant that English law took an evidential, equitable and investigative approach to the exercise of law; but it also meant that owing to the common law system, English law was a fluid and progressive law that based its principles on real life situations.

The Assize of Clarendon gave rise to the common law system that the United Kingdom uses today. This system does not take a purely top-down approach to legislation, but rather acts according to the circumstance. For example, once a decision has been made, this decision is binding on courts of equal or lower authority for all time until Parliament, or a higher court, changes the law. The result of this, is a flexible, pragmatic approach to legislation insofar as the judiciary rules on matters or cases that are 'real'. Contrast this with a civil code, and we see a situation where those at the top must essentially imagine or foresee all possible wrongdoings and legislate for them accordingly. Similarly, the lack of flexibility in a civil code means that judges are not free to interpret the law within the spirit of it, but rather must interpret the law to the letter. This can lead to some rather absurd outcomes where one person's actions are treated as a wrongdoing, whilst another person's similar actions are treated differently because of a slight variation in the circumstance. Civil codes do not examine the intention of the law, nor the intention of the defendant, but rather they focus on the wording of the law in a somewhat far too literal sense.

Surprisingly to some, the crime of murder was never legislated for in Parliament in the United Kingdom. Instead, murder is an example of a common law offence that has come to be through the common law legal system. In the 17th Century Sir Edward Coke defined the murder as:

> "Murder is when a man of sound memory and of the age of discretion, unlawfully killeth within any county of the realm

any reasonable creature in rerum natura under the King's peace, with malice aforthought, either expressed by the party or implied by law, so as the party wounded, or hurt, etc. die of the wound or hurt, etc. within a year and a day of the same[8]."

As a result, the necessary criteria for satisfying the criteria for murder, that is to say the necessary psychological intention, was that the accused was sane, old enough to be held accountable in law for his actions, has killed a human being without legal permission of any kind to do so, did so maliciously, and did so through wounding or hurting the individual to the extent that they died as a result within a year and a day from the act. All of the definitions of each criteria, such as 'unlawful killing' and 'wound or hurt' are also found in various cases and rulings, and thus the crime of murder is one that carries a thorough definition and criteria which is fitting given that it also carries a severe punishment.

The fact that this very serious crime came about through the natural development of common law, demonstrates just how practical and useful the common law system is. It is this pragmatism, which resulted from the Assize of Clarendon, that has set the United Kingdom and other common law jurisdictions apart from the rest; without it, we would perhaps not have had the ingenuity to develop the liberties and freedoms that exist in the 21st century. The common law system allows judges to truly judge a case on its merit and circumstance rather than on some political ambition from the legislature. It is a truly accountable, realistic and smooth legal system, and it is the same legal system that our very own constitution emanates from.

---

[8] Coke, Edward; *the Institutes of the Laws of England*, Part 3, Chapter 7, p. 47, London: Printed by M[iles] Flesher, for W[illiam] Lee and D[aniel] Pakeman, 1644.

The Assize of Clarendon is a constitutional document because it concerns individual liberty, which ultimately pertains to the power that the government or arms thereof, have over the individual. The United Kingdom's legal system today, of which the constitution is a part, has a wonderful and unique ability to adapt to constantly changing circumstances in the world, and to mould itself to the direction that the nation chooses to go without straying from the fundamental principles it is designed to uphold. Contrast this with the United States for example; the Twenty-Seventh Amendment, which concerned a rise in the wages of US politicians, took over 202 years to pass into law! Yes, this may go some way in protecting the nation from rapid changes for which there is no appetite, and indeed it may guard the constitution from interference, it is still fundamentally flawed. In a dynamic world where politics is a global affair and the markets hold so much power over the directions of the wind countries must be able to adapt instantaneously whilst remaining true to their convictions and principles; this is especially important in times of great crisis. For example in 1940, on the same day that Hitler invaded the Low Countries, George VI appointed Churchill Prime Minister, without any election. Imagine for a moment, if some codified constitutional doctrine that prevented the King from doing anything of the sort and insisted upon an election. It is safe to say, that the war would have been lost, and all of our liberties, identity and history with it!

The Assize of Clarendon is responsible for the introduction into the English legal system of a number of principles, doctrines and conventions; all of which form an absolutely crucial part of the United Kingdom's constitution today. Whilst it took many years to fully develop these concepts therefore they did not come to be immediately with the Assize, it did nonetheless create the rock upon which these principles were built. As a result, we owe the birth of not only the common law system itself to the Assize, but also concepts like; the Queen's peace; entering a plea; the granting of bail; evidential trials rather than trial by ordeal or duel; reasonable suspicion; the right to remain silent; and trial by jury.

All of these principles are extremely important, not just as concepts, but in practice, for every single one of us. It is somewhat tragic that so few people realise that the Assize of Clarendon even exists, and that many of the liberties contained therein are still as relevant today as they always were. The reality of the situation is that the more ignorant we allow ourselves to become, the more likely we are to unwittingly hand over these valuable jewels that we have inherited, in return for cheap knock-offs.

It was Oscar Wilde's Lord Darlington who famously claimed that one of his fellow characters, in the novel Lady Windermere's Fan, was; *"a man who knows the price of everything and the value of nothing"*. Sadly, when it comes to liberties, freedoms and the constitution of the United Kingdom, at a time when the European Union debate is dominated by economics and finance (all of which are on the side of the Leave campaign though this is a whole different debate); this statement is as true of society now as it was then.

---

[9] Oscar Wilde, *Lady Windermere's Fan, 1892, Act III*

Dominic Bardill

CHAPTER 4
THE MAGNA CARTA

Whilst the Assize of Clarendon laid down the foundations upon which the modern common law trial, many constitutional principles and individual liberties were built, it was not their final development. Perhaps the most famous constitutional and legal document in the entire world, the Magna Carta was truly ahead of its time. There is no piece of parchment on the planet that was so sharp as to completely cut the shackles of government that had dug itself deep into the skin around the wrists of the English people. The Magna Carta, did not just free the English or British, it provided a new, real and honest concept of liberty and freedom, to the entire world and whomsoever wished to take it. It is unfortunate then, that the Magna Carta is almost never mentioned in this country, not unless there is some anniversary where we blindly talk about how wonderful it is whilst simultaneously signing over powers to countries that still do not understand its concepts to this day and possibly never will.

It is the greatest shame that even in the 21st Century, when the Magna Carta had arguably come to it's true fruition and where most of the country can read and write, there is seemingly an epidemic of ignorance, an almost obliviousness, towards what was perhaps the single greatest achievement of mankind. It is indeed a bold claim to make, what with advances in the scientific, medicinal and technological fields, but it is a claim that I firmly stand by. There is nothing that we have achieved as a civilisation, or that mankind has accomplished, in the entirety of history, that has a further and more enduring reach than the Magna Carta. I say this with the upmost conviction and with the readiness to defend this position. Yet to many, it means nothing; far less at least, than whatever nauseating triviality is currently happening in the Kardashian family, or whether or not fat people should be taxed on their sugar so that the government can buy a few footballs and feel good about themselves. When many think of freedom, they think of the freedom to work and to own property; to not have the state interfere in their daily lives; to have a family; to speak and think freely and openly; to not be arrested and charged without a fair trial; to not be imprisoned unjustly; and many other rights and freedoms. It would be far simpler then, if people knew that they owed all of those freedoms and more to essentially one thing; this glorious and ancient piece of parchment and every sacred word scribbled upon it; the *Magna Carta Libertatum,* the Great Charter of Liberties.

I will not pretend that the Magna Carta necessarily came about purely as a result of some altruistic desire, although an element of that may have rested within it. Indeed, in the original 1215 draft, some of the elements were considered to be so radical that King Henry III had to release it again in 1216, with a few amendments. The Archbishop of Canterbury drafted the original Magna Carta, of 1215, however it did not necessarily address issues of individual freedom for everyday English people, rather instead it addressed the ever-growing divide between Baron and Monarch that existed in England at that time. The Magna Carta was once again issued with new amendments in 1225 in exchange for tax payments, and finally during Edward I's reign the final draft of the Magna Carta was issued and passed into Statute, giving it the effect of an Act of Parliament; again over a dispute concerning taxation. Once again, we see principles that were developed over a long period, constantly and fluidly adapting to the changing environment. It was in this 1297 draft that Edward I reissued and declared a statutory law that the expansion of liberty beyond certain sections of society truly began.

One of the most essential aspects to take note of in the Magna Carta, is in the *Confirmatio* where it provides clarity that the Magna Carta shall hold supremacy over the land;

> *"if any judgement be given from henceforth contrary to the points of the charters aforesaid by the justices, or by any other our ministers that hold plea before them against the points of the charters, it shall be undone, and holden for nought* [10]*."*

In other words; if anyone rules against the liberties that are handed down in the Magna Carta, then it is completely invalid and the decision will be overruled.

Today, the vast majority of the clauses contained within the Magna Carta have been repealed and replaced by Statute, something that continues to stir up a controversial and heated debate in legal circles. Various statutory provisions have enshrined the clauses as separate statutes, but for the most part, whilst the clauses have been repealed, the principles of them have merely been transferred rather than

---

[10] Article 2, *Confirmation Cartarum* [26], October 10, 1297.

destroyed or abolished. The most significant example of this is in the Statute Law Revision Act, which was passed in the 1800s. This Act repealed 17 of the clauses in the Magna Carta, however it was not as horrific an undertaking as one might first assume. Most of the clauses that were repealed were seen by the Parliament of the day to be redundant because they concerned areas of law that were no longer in function. These areas would be those clauses concerning mediaeval tolls and now defunct practices, whilst other areas included clauses that related to concepts covered, or superseded, by other parts of Statute and therefore protected in a different Act of Parliament. As already suggested, much of the liberties and rights were either no longer relevant or were protected in other Statute; it was not simply a case of removing or abolishing certain liberties.

Hence, there are still three clauses that remain in force in the 21st century. These are clauses 1, 13 and 39 & 40 together considered as one. Whilst few in number, they do nonetheless carry enormous importance.

1) The first clause grants freedom to the Church of England and in addition to this, creates the incredibly precious concept of the 'freeborn' individual, of which you are one, and grants that individual all of the preceding liberties, which as we have already established have now been mostly transferred into statute. The first clause says;

> 'FIRST, We have granted to God, and by this our present Charter have confirmed, for Us and our Heirs for ever, that the Church of England shall be free, and shall have all her whole Rights and Liberties inviolable. We have granted also, and given to all the Freemen of our Realm, for Us and our Heirs for ever, these Liberties under-written, to have and to

hold to them and their Heirs, of Us and our Heirs for ever[11]."

Note that you are freeborn, at least, if you are born in the United Kingdom you are freeborn. The collective of individuals that is referred to when the clause says *"all the Freemen of our Realm"* includes you, your family, your friends and anyone else who is born here in the United Kingdom or has citizenship. This is particularly significant because at that time there was no other nation that recognised such freedom and autonomy for the individual, let alone explicitly and expressly granted that individual freedoms and liberties. Once again, England and subsequently the United Kingdom, was demonstrating just how advanced and ahead of her time she was, compared to her neighbours.

9) The ninth clause, which as stated is also still good law in the United Kingdom, concerns the City of London and expanded those principles outwards to other cities, towns, boroughs etc. also.

> *"The city of London shall enjoy all its ancient liberties and free customs, both by land and by water. We also will and grant that all other cities, boroughs, towns, and ports shall enjoy all their liberties and free customs [12]."*

Why is this so significant? Well, for quite a few reasons in fact. Firstly, before this was issued, cities would have to pay for charters, and charters were what granted them recognition, or rather, existence. Without a charter, you couldn't exist as a city. These methods enabled cities to be

---

[11] Article 1, *Magna Carta 1297* -
http://www.bsswebsite.me.uk/History/MagnaCarta/magnacarta-1297.htm
[12] Article 13, *Magna Carta 1297* -
http://www.bsswebsite.me.uk/History/MagnaCarta/magnacarta-1297.htm

rinsed of their cash to an extent that it would essentially bleed them almost dry and thus that would impact on the residents of that city. This clause had the effect of doing away, at least for a large part, with such a system and this granted them with the freedom and autonomy that was required to flourish, as well as some spare pennies. The result? A more successful economy; wealthier citizenry; greater support for the monarchy; better enterprise and entrepreneurialism; improved social cohesion; and much more in addition. It is this clause that we can thank for the incredible business environment that the City of London provides which grants so much inward investment today, and provides millions with well-paying jobs. It is this clause which we can thank for having local government in our area that is able to invest as it sees fit and capitalise on trade and finance. It is this clause that we owe the economic, political, social and in some respects international success of the United Kingdom because it devolved powers in the proper sense, as opposed to the neo-devolution we see today, so that individual cities or towns could run their affairs and have the resources to do so, in line with the interests of those living there. Although I will not claim it always worked that way, the point is that the principle was there, the autonomy was there along with the extra resources, and it was up to the city in question to use it.

39 & 40) The final of the three clauses that are still very much good law in the 21st century pertains to two sections taken as one. The point of address here is, in my opinion, the single most important of the three, because it is the final logical conclusion or endpoint of the direction in which the Magna Carta was moving, and indeed the King was moving, when granting these clauses. It concerns the importance of trial by jury:

"No free man shall be seized or imprisoned, or stripped of his rights or possessions, or outlawed or exiled, or deprived of his standing in any other way, nor will we proceed with force against him, or send others to do so, except by the lawful judgement of his equals or by the law of the land [13].

"To no one will we sell, to no one deny or delay right or justice. No free man shall be seized or imprisoned, or stripped of his rights or possessions, or outlawed or exiled . nor will we proceed with force against him . Except by the lawful judgement of his equals or by the law of the land [14]. "

One would hope that the reason why this is such an imperative principle is plainly obvious to most people. However, erring on the side of caution it is perhaps necessary to point it out. The reason that you cannot merely be accused of wrongdoing by your neighbour and subsequently thrown into a prison cell – like in Saudi Arabia for example, is because of this clause. Finally, the principles lay down in the Charter of Liberties, the Bill of Rights and the Assize of Clarendon were solidified and summarised in this clause; which lives on today with as much breath as it had when it was born. This Charter has formed the basis for numerous civilisations across the English-speaking world such as New Zealand and the United States of America, and it is, at the risk of sounding fantastical, your very freedom.

The Magna Carta protects your individual liberty to such a huge extent and yet it is probably something that was never mentioned to you in school. It has become somewhat of a

---

[13] Article 39, *Magna Carta 1297* -
http://www.bsswebsite.me.uk/History/MagnaCarta/magnacarta-1297.htm
[14] Article 40, *Magna Carta 1297* -
http://www.bsswebsite.me.uk/History/MagnaCarta/magnacarta-1297.htm

historicised concept; regarded as some ancient document from days gone by which we look upon with pride and romance but little else. The reality is, it is as important today as ever, in fact I would argue that given the threats that we face from the European Union towards our liberties, it is even more relevant. Naturally some of these threats will be addressed later on. Primarily, for the moment, if we are to understand just how intricate this seemingly distant Charter is to us as individuals, then it is important not to simply have a memorised version in our minds, but instead to understand the wider concept that ensues from it concerning the liberties of the freeborn individual; or in other words, you.

Note in the last of the quotations of text from the Magna Carta itself above, that it declares some very important points that demonstrate just how sacred and supreme these liberties are. You cannot be imprisoned, deprived of your freedom and liberties, have force used against you, be exiled or lose your standing, without a fair trial by jury. You cannot be denied, delayed or buy your right to justice, or in other words, you are equal before the law and justice is no longer a commodity. These are absolutely vital things. Without them, the United Kingdom would have more in common with North Korea than it does with New Zealand – a terrifying and yet gratitude-inducing prospect. The Magna Carta, together with the Charter of Liberties and the Assize of Clarendon, create not only liberties for the individual and others, but they create an entire perspective of liberty too. This viewpoint underpins the traditional British way of viewing liberty, which is in stark contrast to the way that liberties are upheld, or rather not, on the continent – negative liberty.

Negative liberty is essentially the liberty to do that which is not forbidden. Another way of looking at this kind of liberty is to describe it as asking the question *'where is it written that I cannot?'* as opposed to *'where is it written that I can?'*. In other words, the British concept of liberty is rooted in the attitude that you are free to pursue whatever you wish, provided it is not expressly forbidden; again we see this concept of being born free, or 'freeborn'. Chiefly, negative liberty is the idea that your liberty comes naturally, and thus your rights are prescribed by nature, thus any interference in those rights from an outside or external force such as the government or another individual, is a restriction on those liberties. Negative liberty is concerned with external influence and the prohibition of it in the absence of justification. This means that negative liberty is about having the freedom *from* something, namely external factors, that prevent you from exercising the freedom that you otherwise would naturally have.

In contrast to this, characteristic of most civil law systems, there exists 'Positive Liberty', which rests on the premise that you are free to pursue what you are permitted to pursue; the question is *'where is it written that I can?'* This type of liberty works in the opposite way; rather than being concerned with external restrictions and outside interference, or the protection from them, instead it is concerned with the internal. In other words, positive liberty is about the *freedom to* something. Rights in positive liberty are about having the capacity to do or have something. In practice, it is my belief that this is no liberty at all! Allow me to explain why.

Envisage for a moment, that you wish to learn to play the violin. So you decide to go to a shop and buy a violin to begin learning. Negative liberty would say that you have the right to buy a violin and learn to play it, provided the seller did not exercise his right to refuse, and so if the government or some other individual were to wrap tape around both of your hands to prevent you from being able to play, or imprison you so that you could not go out to buy the violin, then they would be infringing on your liberties. In such a situation, since the state exists in order to protect us, including our liberties, the government would be under an obligation to prevent you from being imprisoned or having your hands taped up. This could be done physically, by using the police to free you from imprisonment, or it can be done through the law, by forbidding anyone from wrongfully imprisoning another, or incapacitating another. Essentially, the job of the government in this regard is simply to protect you from undue interference with your liberties, so that you can get on with whatever you wish. It is about forbidding others, including the state itself, from removing your *capacity* to act as you wish.

Now imagine the same situation, but this time, you are not taped up or imprisoned. Instead, you simply do not have enough money to buy a violin and take lessons, or you do not have Internet access in order to view online tutorials. In this scenario, positive liberty would say that by virtue of the fact that you do not have the *capacity* to exercise your liberty, your liberty is being contravened. The resulting principle of this, is that some may argue that the state has some obligation, since it is charged with protecting your liberties just as before, to provide you with the resources in which to assist you. Providing you with Internet access and a violin, or even violin lessons could do this. Broadly then, positive liberty is not about protecting your capacity from outside interference and disablement, but rather, granting you a capacity that you do not have. It is about giving or ensuring people have the capacity to do something, rather than not taking it away. Naturally this requires a large level of state or external interference in order to 'empower' you to do things.

Logically in the eyes of negative liberty, the less interference in your life the better. Whilst with positive liberty, and I believe this to be a dangerous concept, the state or some outside entity is obliged to interfere in order for those rights to exist. Thus, this is why positive liberty emanates from complete codification of constitutions and laws in a civil law code; it stands to reason that the state must express its obligations or else the obligation to act on the part of the state would be infinite and impossible to uphold. As a consequence of this, the state lists things that you have a right *to* by saying things in a positive manner so as to define what you are entitled to. Since this list cannot go on forever, the end result is full of more pretty words and virtuous sentences, but very little else. The truth is, that it does not grant you or recognise any rights at all, instead it actually grants rights, and power, to the state itself. Think about this for a moment.

Effectively therefore, the difference is a philosophical one. For example, whilst on the face of it both positive and negative liberties are the same, the underlying philosophy or reasoning, which leads to determining what exactly constitutes a right, is where they part. A good way of thinking of a negative liberty is that it is a 'God given' or 'natural' right, or in other words, one you are born with. Whilst on the other hand a positive right is one that you are granted. Due to the fact that negative liberties are about prohibiting those things you *cannot* do and thus leaving you at liberty to do anything that is not forbidden, positive liberty is about permitting what you *can* do and therefore you are only free to do what is permitted.

A great and universally known example of negative liberties in action, is rooted in the 10 Commandments in fact. Take *'Thou shalt not kill'* as an example; it grants you the right to life, by removing another's right to take it. It is not giving you the right to life by granting you the positive right to life, but rather it is giving you the right to life by prohibiting the removal of your life; you are naturally born with the right to life and therefore it is a 'God given' or 'natural' liberty that can only be infringed by someone interfering with it. Compare this to what we now call *'Human Rights'*, in the modern European Union sense of the word, and we see an example of the philosophy behind positive liberty. In the thinking behind human rights, the rights come from the state, and thus it is the state that is somehow appointed the moral arbitrator of what is and is not a right; something that is constantly reviewed and renewed.

Because negative liberty requires no intervention in order for it to be upheld, it truly empowers the individual to have control over their own life; naturally sometimes they may require and indeed be granted help from the state or other means, but the liberty itself is manifest simply by virtue of being a human being who is born free, note again we see this ancient theme of being 'freeborn' that England gave birth to. On the other hand, positive liberty, because it requires permission, it requires state recognition, thus the fact that it emanates from the state means that until it is recognised as a right, it is illegal. Indeed, everything is unlawful or illegal unless the state grants you that right. In my opinion, this is akin to the liberty of a dog that can conduct itself only according to its master's wishes, not the liberty of a human being.

The biggest danger with positive liberty is precisely the nature of state involvement; if you require the state to grant rights, and if the same state has the authority to uphold, review or change them, then the very state on which you rely can easily use it against you. For instance, if the state grants me a right to a house, and then subsequently in upholding that right gives me a house, then life is sweet. However, if the state reviews this and decides that it is not a right to have a house, and so snatches it away, thus ripping my life apart, then how can I complain? In essence then, when I say that positive rights actually grant rights to the state, over the individual, this is what I am trying to illustrate. Your negative liberty entitles you to buy a home and live in it; the state must respect personal property laws – thus granting you rights. Positive liberty acts on the logic that you have an *entitlement* to a house and therefore the state should provide it, but that same right is granted by the state too and not a natural one, consequently the state in the process is granted the right to decide whether you are really entitled to a house, which house and whether or not to take it away. Rights are actually a possession of the state because of the power that it exercises over your rights as a result of positive liberty. The fact that positive liberty actually places liberties in the hands of governments that have a track record of continually ignoring them, should serve as an example of just how superior the truly English, and British, model of liberty is.

Sadly, along with Human Rights -which we will explore shortly- there are many aspects of European Union law that place this valuable principle of negative liberty, which recognises your freeborn nature, in jeopardy. A freeborn nature that many people justifiably died to protect through the centuries, is precious because it gives you sovereignty over yourself, without the interference of any other agent, and yet many people will gladly throw it away in return for positive rights, which as already stated, places you in the position of a child under the guardianship of a parent. It is then no wonder we have grown to be a dependent, irresponsible and uncritical society.

Nevertheless, there is a way that we too can protect and save it, to be cherished, as it should be. Before this though, it is critical to see how all of the previously discussed concepts, contribute to the very existence of the United Kingdom, and her survival, through the greatest constitution in the history of the world.

CHAPTER 5
OUR CONSTITUTION

The United Kingdom's Constitution may arguably be one of the most ancient in the world, but it is also one of the most enduring. It has been formed over centuries; by some of the greatest minds that civilisation has known. John Alder describes the United Kingdom's Constitution as a unique blend of laws and conventions which when put together enable it, through fluidity and pragmatism, to adhere to the demands and requirements of any given age. Alder states:

> *"Our pragmatic mixture of ordinary laws and political conventions is said to have the advantage of practicality in that it responds to particular issues that arise from time to time and can easily adapt to changing circumstances [15]."*

The common law legal system, so popular in the Anglosphere, is an absolutely fundamental tenet of the United Kingdom's Constitution. It follows very much the same system itself, developing in response to various historical events and obstacles in the same way that common law

---

[15] Alder, John; *Constitutional and Administrative Law,* p.9, Palgrave Macmillan, 28th June 2013.

develops along with wrongdoings and situations of the day. The United Kingdom's Constitution has developed over such an enormous and almost incomprehensible period of time, to become one of the oldest, and yet still one of the most relevant and practical constitutions in the world today. Our constitution consists of some of the most famous and important written and unwritten rules, laying claim to such invaluable achievements as Magna Carta, the Assize of Clarendon and the Habeas Corpus, various realistic precedents and conventions, and of course statutory legislation that comes from Parliament. Dicey describes the Rule of Law and Parliamentary Sovereignty as the twin pillars of the UK constitution[16].

Parliamentary Sovereignty involves three principles according to the notable A.V. Dicey; (i) parliament has the power to amend or change any law whatsoever, (ii) no Parliament can be restricted by a predecessor or bind its successor, and (iii) nobody, including the court, may question the validity of Acts of Parliament[17]. The principle of Parliamentary Supremacy or Sovereignty is so engrained and integral to the United Kingdom's legal system, that Sir Leslie Stephen proclaimed, *"If a legislature decided that all blue-eyed babies should be murdered, the preservation of blue-eyed babies would be illegal...[18]"*. Upon first glance it becomes apparent what the various dangers of this kind of system are; authoritarianism, lack of accountability, corruption and even worse. In fact, the United Kingdom has even been referred to by Sir Leslie as an *"Elective Dictatorship[19]"*,

---

[16] *Mark Ryan, Steve Foster*, Unlocking Constitutional & Administrative Law, Routledge, 2013, Page 103.

[17] A.V. Dicey, *Introduction to the Study of the Law of the Constitution* (1885)

[18] Leslie Stephen, *The Science of Ethics*, p. 145 (1882)

[19] Hailsham, *The Dilemma of Democracy*, Ch.20; Scarman, Why Britain Needs a Written Constitution, pp.6–7.

referring to the fact that even though the United Kingdom's legislative Chamber is an elected one, once it has been elected, it constitutionally holds absolute authority and supremacy. It is without doubt a perfectly reasonable and realistic phobia, to fear a government with unlimited power and with no means of recourse.

Whilst with the United Kingdom's constitution, sovereignty is placed in the hands of Parliament, which raises perfectly valid questions regarding power, countries with codified constitutions, in which the constitution is a single written entity, have rather a different approach; theoretically at least. When a constitution is codified, the general norm is that Sovereignty lies with its citizens, which is a potentially clearer and democratic method of constitutional governance. Note I use the word potentially, because as any wise man knows, the pursuit of an ideal does not always end with the desired result.

In 1958, the current Constitution of the Republic of France was born. It is worth noting that this is not their first constitution, since they are currently on their fifth republic; evidently it is working out exceptionally well for them. It is nonetheless their current constitution, and it makes the source of sovereignty abundantly clear when it declares that; *"National sovereignty shall vest in the people, who shall exercise it through their representatives and by means of referendum[20]."* It wouldn't be entirely unreasonable then, if we were to go based purely on words and ignore all possible ulterior motives or token gestures that might play a part, to assume that contrary to an uncodified constitution, the chance of a government ignoring the demands of its people, is

---

[20] *The French Constitution of October 4, 1958*, Title 1, Article 3.

eliminated by virtue of those words that invest the sovereignty into them. Provisions like that do not, and moreover cannot exist in the United Kingdom. Not, at least, under the current constitution, if we to wish to remain loyal to it, which undoubtedly we absolutely should.

If the United Kingdom wanted to adopt a codified constitution similar to that of France, or the majority of other countries on the planet with the exception of Israel and New Zealand, who have a similar system to us, then much would have to change. We would need to introduce 'Higher' or 'Superior' laws that went above Parliament itself. Which would be an outright abolition of Parliamentary sovereignty or supremacy. At present there is no such legal restriction on Parliament, of course there isn't, it is a sovereign and supreme Parliament as far as the constitution and legal system is concerned. Introducing a set of higher laws would place restrictions on Parliament - indeed this would be the very purpose of those laws. The Parliament Acts 1911[21] and 1949[22] permit the House of Commons to force legislation through the House of Lords, and the Succession to the Crown Act 2013[23] demonstrates how Parliament can make changes to fundamental conventions regarding the succession to the throne. These kinds of statutes show us how limitless the capabilities of the United Kingdom's Parliament are under our uncodified constitutional system. On the other hand, 'entrenchment' is usually used in a codified system, which is designed to protect the constitution of the respective country,

---

[21] Parliament Act 1911 - http://www.legislation.gov.uk/ukpga/Geo5/1-2/13/contents

[22] Parliament Act 1949 - http://www.legislation.gov.uk/ukpga/Geo6/12-13-14/103/contents

[23] Succession to the Crown Act 2013 -
http://www.legislation.gov.uk/ukpga/2013/20/section/1

something that does not exist in the United Kingdom. If the United Kingdom were to adopt a codified system, it would need to entrench its higher laws in order to protect them from government meddling. This would involve placing within a law, the method by which that law might be changed. For example, passing a Bill that governs the salary conditions of parliament, and within that law placing the requirement that any change can only take place with a two-thirds majority in both Houses, would be an example of entrenchment. These additional requirements, remove the possibility for governments to make changes to the constitutional code of the country too easily, by placing a lengthier, and strenuous process in front of it; evidently this is unnecessary and impossible in a country without a codified constitution, such as the United Kingdom. The French constitution contains the provision; *"The republican form of government shall not be the object of any amendment.*[24] *"* which is a very clear example of entrenchment in action. This type of added element of security is often seized on as a useful argument by those who either advocate a codified position, or are critical of uncodified constitutions. In fact, the United Kingdom has floated the idea of introducing a codified constitution before, with Blair's Labour Government holding a consultation and releasing a report. Nevertheless, this did not materialise, thankfully so!

You may be pondering why on earth I would demonstrate the theoretical advantages of a codified constitution, whilst simultaneously speaking against any introduction of one. It may appear confusing for someone who believes in liberty and individual freedoms, to oppose a system that would essentially protect the very code that governs the

---

[24] The French Constitution of October 4, 1958, Title 16, Article 89.

government, and moderates the relationship between government and people. That is because I feel it necessary to look beyond mere theory and words, into practice. What are the practical, material results of a codified or uncodified constitution? We looked before at the French constitution, so we will look there again. The aforementioned example of an entrenched clause regarding the French Constitution, where it states that; *"The republican form of government shall not be the object of any amendment[25]."* renders any possible amendment to the type of political or government structure in France, to be impossible, at least without starting a sixth republic, which would be rather embarrassing. Nevertheless, is it not true then, that this directly conflicts with the initial article concerning where sovereignty lies? If sovereignty rests in the French people, and the French people were to demand a Monarchy for example, then a constitutional crisis would surely ensue and as mentioned before, a revolution and a demolition of the 1958 constitution in favour of a new order would be necessary. The reality is however, that the government would simply point to the constitution and continue as before, ignoring the wishes of those who they are supposed to represent. This would fundamentally and somewhat paradoxically be a case of the French government, which the constitution is designed to limit, instead using it to empower themselves over the French people so as to authorise ignoring them, and in turn breaching their sovereignty. The great paradox, in my opinion, lies in the fact that the government is able to use a codified document designed to limit their power and place power into the hands of the populous, to instead limit the people and empower themselves.

---

[25] The French Constitution of October 4, 1958, Title 16, Article 89.

This is an example of the practical effect of a codified constitution, and it is not an unusual occurrence. Codifying a constitution does not therefore result in more accountability by definition. In fact, it can provide something for the government to hide behind in order to avoid being accountable altogether. The French people of 2016 did not express any desire or grant any mandate for the constitution of 1958, and yet the document vests sovereignty in them. It seems to me, that real sovereignty seems to lie in the government, who enjoy the added protection of entrenchment to avoid responsibility. The sovereignty, in a codified republic like France, lies in theory with the French people, but not in practise. Entrenchment does not provide accountability, because it removes responsibility. It is no more democratic or sovereign just by virtue of being written down, as it is to suggest that I would be a rich man should I write five million pounds on a piece of blank paper. As an idea it may be wonderful, but in practice it achieves quite the opposite of the 'official' desired result.

Our own uncodified constitution is capable of fluid and fast change, allowing it to adapt quickly to the wishes of the people, changing socio-political climates, or desperate circumstances. Consequently, whilst it is Parliament that is Sovereign and supreme constitutionally, it is through the various conventions and instruments of the United Kingdom's constitution, that this Parliament is compelled to pay much more attention to the wishes of the public. Naturally, Parliament does not always do what the people want, like any country, there is always some degree of alienation, or various areas with which people are not in agreement with the government. Nevertheless, the principle remains that if a government or parliament pushes against the will of the people, in a country like the United Kingdom, then firstly, they will be held accountable for it themselves and unable to point to any codified shield that aids them in passing the buck. Secondly, the result of this would be that the public can remove them, and are likely to remove them, because of the lack of resources such as codified constitutional documents, for the politicians to use to their own advantage. In 1997 The Scottish public voted in a pre-legislative referendum regarding devolution of powers to a Scottish parliament[26], which resulted in the passing into law of the Scotland Act 1998[27]. This is one of numerous examples of the type of pragmatic advantage that an uncodified constitution gives. Parliament was never compelled to pass this law legally, nor were they bound by any statutory instrument to do so. Furthermore, they were not prevented from doing so despite their best wishes, and it did not take a lifetime to organise. It was ultimately, convention in action.

The United Kingdom has elections each term, which poses a risk to any government who wishes to go too far in ignoring or overruling the will of the people. Moreover, due to the structure of Parliament, should a government try to ignore Parliament's wishes or Acts of Parliament that have been passed; there is the risk of a vote of no confidence, which would cause the resignation of the Government and the dissolution of Parliament by the Monarch. Neville Chamberlain for example, resigned after winning a Motion of no Confidence but failing to form a government[28]. Additionally, there could also theoretically be potential criminal issues by virtue of the fact that

---

[26] http://www.scotland.gov.uk/About/Factfile/18060/11550
[27] Scotland Act 1998, http://www.legislation.gov.uk/ukpga/1998/46/contents
[28] http://www.bbc.co.uk/history/events/churchill_becomes_prime_minister

Parliament has passed a law; it is not necessary for an extra codification of superior laws to govern individual politicians, because whilst they are governed constitutionally by convention and principles, they are governed as individuals by the same law as everyone else. Ignoring an Act of Parliament and thus potentially breaking the law carries the same consequences for a Minister as it does for the average Joe on the street. Consequently, there are a whole host of various genuine, practical and fluid checks & balances that keep the political elite in check; certainly not completely perfectly, but more perfectly than any other nation with a codified constitution.

The United States has more or less the same common law system that the United Kingdom adopts, but maintains a codified constitution, perhaps even one of the most famous. In the constitution of the USA, there is the method of impeachment in dealing with Presidents who breach it. In the event of an impeachment, the accused is tried in a trial over which The Chief Justice presides. Perhaps in this system, whereby the President is directly and individually responsible for his actions provides more accountability. What President would dare to subvert the constitution and principles of a nation when legal or civil action casts a dark shadow as it leers over his shoulder and scrutinises his every movement? What President, with such grand cannons pointed at him, or her, would nonetheless choose to rally against their own country? Well, I can perhaps answer that. The answer depends on just how much substance there is behind the process or the principle. If, as in the French case, it does little more than pay lip service, then any savvy President would be fully aware of this and what he needs to do in order to get away cleanly and easily. Sadly, for the United States, it is very much little more than lip service, just like in the French case and indeed much like in the case of numerous other countries across the planet —Brazil being a very recent example. How does one know that for the most part impeachment is any more effective than a sword made of sugar glass?

Well, when the formal process of impeachment takes place, as mentioned before, the Chief Justice presides over the trial of the accused Government Minister. However, who chooses the Chief Justice? By what method does he obtain his office? At whose hand and authority? Well, as you probably assumed, the President nominates his preferred and chosen candidate to be Chief Justice, and the Senate then appoints this individual by virtue of a confirmation vote[29]. Ask yourself, is it still genuinely accountable? Or does this not bring into question the validity of the very process itself? In fact, since the very first election in the then newly created USA right through to the present day, the President has always commanded a majority in the Senate. This means that those who are confirming the President's choice are unlikely to oppose him and would effectively 'tow the line' and approve of whoever is nominated. Naturally mid-term elections can have an impact on this, since it is often during this period that Presidents lose popularity, but this is why new members of the judiciary are appointed at the start of a new term. Why do you think it is the case that upon the death of the admirable Supreme Court Judge Antonin Scalia, the Republicans sought to delay the appointment of a new judge until after the 2016 elections, whilst the Democrats wished to do so immediately? It is simple; both sides want

---

[29] United States Constitution, Article 1, Section 3,

to hold the balance of power when it comes to nominating and confirming someone for appointment to such a prestigious seat in the judiciary. A similar situation regarding judiciary appointments and impeachment, amongst other instruments, are prevalent in most countries where there is a codified constitution –essentially these are normal and expected methods in such countries.

In the United Kingdom however, impeachment cannot and does not need to exist. Consequently, there is rarely ever a situation where the judiciary and constitution become so politicised so as to warrant the treatment of a part political punch bag, worthy of tactics and representing little more than an opportunity for politicians to exercise their influence. It seems to me, that a codified constitution does not keep the government or politicians in check any more than stringent tax legislation successfully prevents money laundering and tax evasion. This is because whilst is may be true that just like money laundering and tax evasion, the more codified and buried in strictly aligned 'provisions' that legislation becomes, the less room there is to maneuver, it presents a difficulty when it is the people who wish to do the maneuvering. In other words, it often restricts those who wish to hold government to account, much more than the government itself, and perhaps this is because, just like tax evasion and money laundering, there is often a way for those at the top to work around it or bend it in their favour. Instead of such methods as impeachment or other legal repercussions, the United Kingdom takes a rather a different approach, and arguably a much more natural one; convention. It is through the use of conventions that the United Kingdom keeps its politicians in line –again not perfectly; although compared to many foreign politicians we really do get off lightly.

There are myriad conventions that form part of the United Kingdom's constitution, and since by their very nature they are not written down or codified, they are virtually impossible to pin down all at once in one place, but you would know one if you saw it in action. In order to illustrate what a convention is, let us look at two conventions that would come to be useful in a situation where a codified constitution would demand impeachment. These two conventions are the conventions of Individual Ministerial Responsibility and Collective Ministerial Responsibility.

The UK's use of convention does not fully allow for this. In the UK constitution it would be the conventions of Individual and Collective Ministerial Responsibility. Individual Ministerial responsibility, which does not actually rule out criminal trials for Ministers anyway, means that each Minister is individual responsible for his own conduct and his department. Consequently, if he fails to do his job or behave properly he will resign, to preserve the government. Furthermore, he is the public face of his department, and accountable directly to Parliament for the actions of it.

Furthermore, Individual Ministerial Responsibility allows for a wide maintenance of standards in that because it is based not on law, but on behaviour and conduct and the political loss attached to it, it extends to governance of the everyday conduct of the Minister. Collective Ministerial Responsibility requires all Ministers to present a united front in public; enabling them to speak more honest and freely in private but command the confidence and unity of the nation in public, giving greater stability. For example,

Baroness Warsi recently resigned over the government's policy on Israel and Palestine, this is an example of Collective Ministerial Responsibility, as her resignation is the conventional way of standing for individual principles, without causing the whole government to fall. This again, is a pragmatic and practical use of convention to promote accountability[30].

Aside from the fact that an uncodified constitution appears to give greater accountability through conventions, there is also an issue of flexibility. As Alder mentions above, the UK constitution has an ability to adapt to new issues and changing circumstance. In the US Constitution, the Twenty-Seventh Amendment took just over 202 years to pass[31]. Whilst this is useful for preventing rapid and unwanted change or interference to a constitution, it has its drawbacks; in an ever-changing world it is important for countries to be able to adapt instantaneously. In 1940, on the same day that Hitler invaded the Low Countries, George VI appointed Churchill Prime Minister[32], with no election. If it were not for the important convention of Parliamentary Sovereignty, and if the UK constitution had been codified in a similarly rigid manner to that of France, the Monarch would potentially have had no legal right to appoint Churchill, or the process would have been a longer and more drawn out one such as in the example of the USA above. Consequently, a huge positive of an uncodified constitution is its ability to adapt to an important and fast

---

[30] Channel 4 News: *Baroness Warsi Quits Government over Gaza'* [5TH August 2014], Retrieved 2nd May 2016; http://www.channel4.com/news/warsi-baroness-resignation-gaza-government-policy

[31] http://libres.uncg.edu/ir/asu/f/Strickland_Ruth_Ann_1993_The_Twenty_Seventh.pdf

[32] http://www.bbc.co.uk/history/events/churchill_becomes_prime_minister

paced world, and the way in which it is pragmatic and fluid, the appointment of Churchill and subsequent salvation of Europe, as well as the wider world, being a direct example of Alder's quote in action.

Critics of an uncodified constitution would still argue that this is undemocratic. The convention of a Monarch being allowed to appoint whoever they wish as Prime Minister, is simply not good enough whether that right is exercised or not. In theory, yes, it is undemocratic, at least in a very broad sense; however as with the case of individual and collective ministerial responsibility, due to the separation of Government through the Judiciary, Executive and Legislature, one can argue that the survival of each depends on the scrutiny of each other, and the UK constitution allows them to work against each other, but also in tandem when the need arises, because it is convention that governs them.

In fact, there have been recent efforts to reform Parliament; in 2014, Ed Milliband announced an intention to create a Senate to replace the House of Lords[33]. Many believe this would be more democratic. Nevertheless, since the Constitutional Reform Act 2005 the justices of the UK courts are appointed by the Judicial Appointments Commission, which is made up of laypeople, judges, legal professionals, lay justices and tribunal members[34]. This demonstrates a clear necessity and inevitable involvement of non-elected aspects of the constitution, even in the case of a Senate. As a result, even in a codified constitution it

---

[33] BBC NEWS; *Elected Senate would replace House of Lords under Labour;* [1st November 2014], Retrieved 30th April 2016, - http://www.bbc.co.uk/news/uk-politics-29857849
[34] Constitutional Reform Act 2005 -
http://www.legislation.gov.uk/ukpga/2005/4/contents

would be necessary to have a Constitutional or Administrative Court, the difference being that due to a lack of Parliamentary Sovereignty, the courts could strike down laws it deems unconstitutional. This, in essence, could lead to judicial tyranny, creating either potential for political interference in the judiciary, or Judicial Sovereignty rather than Parliamentary.

Another argument for a codified constitution is that is can enshrine values, standards and rights in law. The Second Amendment of the US constitution; the right to bear arms, was created in 1791, and can be found in the Bill of Rights[35]. At the time, there was arguably a case for including the right to keep and bear arms. However, in 2009, a time of little chance for foreign invasions or rebellions, guns and firearms made up 67% of homicides[36], clearly not something this amendment was intended to enable. Yet to change it would require a long and drawn out process. Contrast this with the United Kingdom, who also has a Bill of Rights, which became the inspiration for that of the USA's own Bill. In the UK, after the Dunblane Massacre in 1996, gun laws were dramatically reformed and quickly implemented through the Firearms (Amendment) Act 1997[37]. All that was required to change the constitution was for an Act of Parliament to be passed in the same way as any other Act. This is a direct example of the fusion between law and political convention; the convention allows Parliament to use its sovereignty to quickly pass a law that it believes is in the interests of the people. Gun

---

[35] http://www.archives.gov/exhibits/charters/bill_of_rights_transcript.html
[16] *Homicides by firearms UNODC Report. Retrieved: 28 July 2012*

[37] Firearms Amendment Act 1997 -
http://www.legislation.gov.uk/ukpga/1997/5/contents

crime in the United Kingdom accounted for just 2.4% of homicides in 2009[38], a dramatic difference compared to the USA, although I would argue that there are a number of other factors involved here too. The point in this example is not about whether or not you agree with gun restrictions, but rather a way of highlighting an example of the UK constitution responding to issues that arise, in the way that it wishes, and adapting to a change of circumstance of its own accord, through its Parliament which is accountable electorally to the public. This, in essence, demonstrates that codification can in fact inhibit progression and staple it in time so that eventually it becomes outdated, whilst an uncodified constitution such as ours is not ancient and outdated, but timeless and fluid in the best possible way.

Moreover, what happens when constitutions contain elements that are in fact detrimental to the people? Another benefit of the United Kingdom's uncodified constitution concerns the way that it has done a magnificent job of protecting us from tyranny, at least compared to other nations across the world. Those people who advocate codified constitutions as a means of great control or restriction of the government seem to forget that the Nazi's even used a codified constitution[39], and Saudi Arabia's equivalent of a constitution states that *"...all members of each family in Saudi Arabia shall be reared "on the basis of the Islamic faith.[40]"* An unequivocal example of restriction of religion enshrined in codification, and therefore inflexible to any

[38] *International firearm injury prevention and policy* -
http://www.gunpolicy.org/firearms/region/united-kingdom
[39] SHOAD Resource Centre; *Compendium of the constitutional laws and principles of Nazi Ideology ("Weltanshauung")* – (PDF Format:
http://www.yadvashem.org/odot_pdf/microsoft%20word%20-%205614.pdf)
[40] *Saudi Arabia Constituton,* Adopted: March 1992 by Royal decree of King Fahd, ICL Document Status: October 1993 - http://www.servat.unibe.ch/icl/sa00000_.html

kind of adaptation or change, at least not without violence and bloodshed. These issues simply do not arise in an uncodified constitution where all laws are passed through Parliament and Parliament's existence is dependent on the electorate and the other agents of government, all limited by convention.

Consequently, it is fair to come to the conclusion that codified constitutions do in fact hinder progress. Evidently, countries with codified constitutions have usually had a catastrophic event leading to some sort of call for it. However, the very fact that the UK has never had such an event rendering it necessary, demonstrates how well the constitution functions in our Kingdom. An uncodified constitution allows the people to be ruled by consent, striking a balance between the judiciary, the executive and the legislature. Rather than being built brick by brick, it has grown like a forest, slowly over time, seemingly chaotic, but following clear principles with each one reliant on the next. I believe it has been shown that the UK constitution's timeless nature, is not only the reason it still exists today, but is also the reason that the United Kingdom more than any other nation, has built modern democracy as a concept, and pioneered the liberties and freedoms most of the world take for granted.

The United Kingdom's constitution is extraordinary; it has been able to develop, evolve and address dangerous emergencies in history, public demands for change, and above all, has united the nation far more than most codified countries could ever dream of. The UK constitution goes beyond mere codification by employing law to enshrine that, which must be enshrined, but maintaining the capacity to review and renew itself, or adapt throughout history, in accordance with national interest, using convention. Britain's mix of written and unwritten law or conventions has created a flexible approach beyond simple law, cementing values held dear internationally earlier on than most, and so has always been ready to meet challenges and address issues before anyone else. It could be the reason why throughout most of history, Britain has often been 10 steps ahead of everyone else.

CHAPTER 6
THE SUPREMACY OF EU LAW

The case of *Factortame*, established the 'doctrine of supremacy' in European Union law as it was ruled that European Law has supremacy over all domestic law[41]. Consequently, when the judge ruled in *Factortame*, it was expressed that where domestic law and European law conflict, the domestic court must always give priority to the European law. Whilst *Factortame* is considered the landmark case, the doctrine of 'Supremacy of EU Law' has been reinforced numerous times (in case the obsession with power wasn't evident enough). It can be seen in cases such as; *Costa v ENEL* where the judge stated; *"...the Members States have limited their sovereign rights...[42]"*, or in *Van Gend en Loos* where it was declared that; *"...the Community constitutes a new legal order of international law for the benefit of which the states have limited their sovereign rights[43]"*. It does not matter what that

---

[41] R v Secretary of State for Transport ex parte Factortame Ltd (No. 7) [2000] EWHC Technology 179 (27 November 2000)

[42] Flaminio Costa v ENEL (1964) Case 6/64

[43] Van Gend en Loos v Nederlandse Administratie der Belastingen (1963) Case 26/62

law is, how it came to be or what the often absurd results are; the European Union's law is supreme over our own, even though it will have come about through some questionable and unaccountable means, as we will explore.

In the United Kingdom Constitution, like many other constitutions, there are several instruments or bodies that serve a particular purpose —albeit that the purpose is not always a clear one. With regards to the United Kingdom constitution, there is the legislature, and the executive. The United Kingdom's Parliament, which is constitutionally sovereign, is the primary legislature in the UK Constitution, which is why it is sovereign and supreme over all others. It is bicameral, with the two Chambers made up of The House of Commons and The House of Lords. Contrary to what many people think, the Monarch also forms part of Parliament, and at present is otherwise known as 'The Queen-in-Parliament'. Each of these three bodies; Commons, Lord and Monarch, make up the United Kingdom Parliament, and each holds an immensely important position, which -when understood, makes perfect sense democratically and pragmatically.

The House of Commons is what would be known as the lower House, literally called the House of Commons because it houses 'commoners'. This term is not meant to be some kind of derogatory insult towards the elected or their electorate, but rather an expression that these men and women are to represent the 'common person', particularly the common people and common interests of those people. Sadly, of course, these representatives have become increasingly self-interested, often doing more to represent their own interests and the interests of those who lobby them. The job of the House of Commons is to make, unmake, approve and disapprove of legislation. Any member of the House of Commons, whether they are in the government or not, may introduce a Bill to Parliament as a means of trying to pass some legislation. This Bill then goes through an arguably thorough process where it is debated, voted on, and amended in various ways before it is finally passed through the House.

The House of Lords is the United Kingdom's upper House. It consists of a wide cross-section of individuals, who are often appointed by a Committee or by the Monarch. In history the members of this House would have most likely inherited their titles and positions, however this is far less so in modern times. What the House does consist of however, are such esteemed people as highly acclaimed scientists, theologians, politicians, engineers, business people, and a whole host of other individuals who have achieved some exceptional goal in their lives or careers. Admittedly, there are those who have been appointed because of cronyism, indeed one would be a fool to deny this, however despite the huge exaggerations in the media about the House of Lords, it is nonetheless mostly occupied by people who are established in their field, and chosen for this reason, rather than by election. The House of Lords may not be perfect, and it has certainly had its fair share of scandals, however with the scandals in the Commons vastly outnumbering that of the Lords, it's safe to say that it is not the nature of appointment or election that is the problem, nor is it a problem unique to the House of Lords, but is rather one of those issues that arises out of a system built by flawed man, operated by flawed man and occupied by flawed man. Nevertheless, putting the debate over the House of Lords to one side, one can still safely assert that the power of the

House of Lords is much more limited, by virtue of the fact that they have been appointed due to an expertise, rather than elected at the will of the people. Consequently, the job of the House of Lords is for the most-part one of scrutiny.

Now imagine for a moment, if we reversed the United Kingdom's Parliament so that it effectively worked backwards with regards to legislative processes and powers. Imagine, if instead of the House of Lords being merely a body of scrutiny, accountability and reporting, it was the main law-making chamber, with the power to pass law, repeal law, and exercise supremacy over the country. Imagine also, that the Commons, rather than being the law-making body, instead occupied the powers of the House of Lords. That is, the power to scrutinise, the power to recommend amendments and the capacity to compile reports and verbally object —no actual law making powers at all. Imagine if the roles of the Commons and the roles of the Lords were reversed, so that now those who represent the 'common man' had no power to make or break law, whilst those who were appointed without election, such as former politicians, which many have complained are recently flooding into the House of Lords, were the lawmakers. Ask yourself, how would you feel about this? How would you feel if the government were to announce that from now on laws will be made by an unelected, appointed body; whilst the scrutiny will come from your elected representatives.

It would, by all objective criteria, be a complete subversion of democracy and every principle that underpins it. Certainly, it is perfectly valid to have unelected elements as part of a wider structure, which provide for accountability (and therefore should not rest on votes) and scrutiny.

Nevertheless, to hand over legislative supremacy to that unelected element, is a step from democracy and accountability, over to authoritarianism and dictatorship. I am quite sure, assuming you are a reasonable and sane individual, that if this were to happen in the United Kingdom, you would join millions of others as they descend onto Parliament in a righteous craze of self-defence at such an attack on your fundamental voice in governance. Yet despite this certainty of mine that you would be nothing short of appalled, this is exactly what has happened!

Of course by that I do not mean that the House of Lords has become the law-making body of Parliament. In fact, the House of Lords is almost the only one of the two Houses that does provide any real objectivity in modern British democracy. When I say that it has already happened, what I mean is that your elected representatives, in Westminster and in the European Parliament, have been reduced to nothing more than flimsy, hollow, papier-mâché versions of their predecessors. The House of Commons is still, at least constitutionally, the primary law-making body in Parliament. Indeed it is the House of Commons who introduce, pass and repeal all of the laws that govern the United Kingdom (notwithstanding those that have been passed to the respective regional assemblies). Indeed the House of Lords is still largely a body of reference and scrutiny, and the Monarch is still required to sign legislation into law. Nevertheless, there is an extra element that no constitutional doctrine in the United Kingdom was ever designed for.

The extra element, that renders the aforementioned scenario to be true, is of course the European Union legislature. In the European Union, it is the EU Commission that makes laws, repeals laws and passes laws. The Commission is made up of 15 individuals who are not elected by the peoples of Europe, but are instead appointed by the various Heads of Government in each member state. This is often done with some agenda in mind, and so of course Britain's influence is often somewhat diminished when placed in a large group of nations with a different outlook, different set of principles and ideals, and a different intention.

Now, you may be wondering then, what is the purpose of these EU Parliamentary Elections that take place in every member state? We all go out and vote, or at least a tiny proportion of us do, and consequently we elect a representative to the EU Parliament to speak for our region. Surely that representative has some control or say over the way that the European Union legislation is introduced, and the way that Europe is governed? Surely that is evidence of the fact that the European Union is a benevolent and democratic institution, driven by the will of its people. Well, at the risk of being the bearer of bad news, you are unfortunately sorely mistaken. Not unreasonably though!

For instance, it would not be unreasonable to assume that when one elects a representative to any kind of parliament, they speak for you and vote on your behalf. It is not unreasonable to assume that when they vote, their vote counts for something, which in turn brings value to your vote, which placed them in that position to begin with. It is not unreasonable, because it is what any reasonable person would expect to be a consequence of any type of electoral parliamentary representation. That is of course, the very reason why it could never be claimed that your assumptions would be unreasonable, indeed they would be absolutely correct if we were talking about a real democratic system, but we are not. Consequently, in spite of common sense, if you thought that your MEPs were there to influence EU legislation on behalf of their voters, then you would nevertheless be absolutely wrong.

In reality, the EU Parliament is nothing short of a rubberstamp parliament designed to give the impression that voters are being heard. Whilst it has the vote on some issues, its vote is either not regarded or cancelled out by the Council of Ministers and European Commission. It holds no real influence over the law-making process in the European Union and is in essence a mere tiny voice amongst great, amplified chants to the contrary. What is most worrying about the legislative and executive setup, or governmental structure of the European Union, is the uncanny similarities that it has with another Union, which represents a darker, painful age in human history. The USSR.

It may sound extreme, but it is nonetheless relevant and accurate to note this point. The USSR was known for its corruption, and was responsible for the systematic oppression of 'inferior' states under its jurisdiction, as well as the oppression of liberties for millions of individuals living under its regime. It was governed by the *Supreme Soviet of Russia;* 'Soviet' meaning 'Council' in English. It's executive, or government, was known -quite worryingly, as *The Council of Ministers* and it is mirrored almost exactly like the Council of Ministers that we see in the European Union today; made up of those representing various regions or areas. The USSR's parliament consisted of two

Chambers; one being the *Soviet of Nationalities*, which was there to represent the different nationalities or regions, much like the European Union Parliament; the other was known Soviet of Russia, which was made up of those who were elected based on the population, by the Council of Ministers, in exactly the same way that the European Union Commission is chosen. There were then smaller, assembly-like governments, which were based in each of the regions or states of the Soviet Union, who sat below the Supreme Soviet in the pecking order.

In essence then, the placing of European Courts above our own domestic courts, the granting of ability of the European Union to simply make laws, the method in which those laws are made and the lack of accountability attached to the structure of all of this, makes the European Union one of the least democratic institutions of the modern era. Moreover, it actually renders the United Kingdom's Parliament nothing more than an obsolete assembly that rules only on those things it has permission to rule on. It makes the United Kingdom parliament as much as 'Micky Mouse' Parliament as the European Parliament is. If your Parliament is not free, or has merely a 'potential' supremacy that is temporarily suspended, then you are not free either; there is no other way to view it.

The exact percentage of the United Kingdom's law and regulation that is in reality governed from Brussels is a topic of fierce debate between pro and anti EU campaigners. Eurosceptic MP Bill Cash claims that 50% of economic laws in the United Kingdom derive from the European Union[44], whilst Polly Toynbee, an outspoken

---

[44] Bill Cash MP (Conservative), House of Commons, 24 October 2011

Europhile, claims that it is just 9% of law in totality that is influence by Brussels[45]. Interestingly, Chuka Umuna, a new Labourite Europhile, claims that around 50% of *"all new regulation"* come from the European Union[46]; the reason this is so interesting is merely because 50% is actually closest to the real figure, so it suggests that Umuna is quite close to actually telling the truth about something –I am of course most surprised by this! Nonetheless, these massively varied figures largely come from the hugely complicated nature of European Law, and thus the method of calculating it. One useful reference for gaining a better idea of how many laws actually do come from Brussels is from an analysis that was carried out on that very subject by the House of Commons Library. In this analysis, the House of Commons Library concluded that up to 50% of UK Law is influenced by or derives from the European Union[47].

Nevertheless, suppressing one's desire to express utter astonishment that any foreign body should be able to simply dictate even 5% of law, down from an unelected, unmovable, and unaccountable body, to the United Kingdom, I will make a simple point. How can the European Union's laws and institutions have supremacy over an apparently sovereign and supreme Parliament?

Of all the conventions, doctrines and legal concepts that the United Kingdom pioneered, Parliamentary Supremacy is the most important because it is the ultimate source of all

---

[45] Toynbee, Polly; *'This Tory rebellion over Europe tells us nothing we don't already know'*, 24th October 2011, The Guardian, Retrieved 30 April 2016 -
http://www.theguardian.com/commentisfree/2011/oct/24/tory-rebellion-europe
[46] "EU legislation...accounts for around half of all new regulation." Chuka Umunna MP, Labour Party press release, 25 October 2011.

[47] House of Commons Library; *'How much legislation comes from Europe?'*, Research Paper 10/62, 13th October 2010.

of those things. How then, can European Law, Parliaments, Commissions and Courts, exercise supremacy over us, without our own Parliament throwing away all that it was placed to protect? There is a case to be made that Parliamentary Sovereignty is so undermined by the doctrine of EU Supremacy, as are our courts and institutions, that our constitution now only exists in principle, but no longer in practice. I believe this is intentional. If a nation's Parliament is imprisoned, so too are the people and since the European Union is about power; this is precisely the European Union's intention.

CHAPTER 7
THE 'NEW CONSTITUTIONS'

Treaties are a long established element of International Law and constitute legally binding agreements between nation states covering a wide variety of areas and themes. The Treaty of Versailles for example is a famous treaty which marked the end of World War I; the Treaty of Utrecht made Gibraltar a British Overseas Territory and the Treaty of Ghent was the treaty that 'officially' ended the war between the United Kingdom and the USA in 1814 (the Battle of New Orleans still went ahead two weeks afterwards partially due to the time it took for news to reach various geographical locations in that age).

In terms of the European Union, treaties have direct effect, which you will now understand sufficiently. There are two treaties that stand out as being those on which the European Union as we know it today was founded and which concern us as individuals quite significantly. The first is the *Maastricht Treaty*, or *The Treaty on the European Union (TOEU)* as it is properly called, the second being *the Treaty of Rome*, or *the Treaty for the Functioning of the European Union*.

The Maastricht Treaty (TOEU)

Brought into effect in 1993, this treaty established the very basis for the modern European Union, taking it from the Common Market and moving it towards a political and social union; a journey that continues to this very day. In fact, it is summarised most simply and clearly in Article G where it states that the Maastricht Treaty is not so much a brand new concept, but a continuous one. It is ultimately an amendment of an older concept that stems from the Treaty Establishing the European Economic Community; the treaty that initially created the Common Market. The Maastricht Treaty makes this clear in the words. Hence, Article G lays out the amendments that are to be made to that treaty in order to establish the new Maastricht Treaty. Article G declares that:

> *"The Treaty establishing the European Economic Community shall be amended in accordance with the provisions of this Article, in order to establish a European Community* [48]. *"*

To make the point even clearer, in Article G (A) (1) where it makes it quite clear that with this treaty we are seeing the Common Market expand well beyond the purpose for which it was apparently created, and into an entirely new realm. The words; *"The term 'European Economic Community' shall be replaced by the 'European Community' "* demonstrate just how blatant the intentions are! No longer are we the Common Market to which the British people agreed in their 1975 referendum; rather, we have removed the word 'economic' altogether, thereby marking the moment at

---

[48] Article G, *Treaty on European Union* OJ C 191, 29.7.1992, p. 1–112

which the community ceases to be about trade alone, and instead the European Union is born.

Naturally, it is a lengthy and complex piece of legislation that cannot be listed and micro analysed in its entirety in one single book. However, since we are focusing here on the contradictions and conflicts that European Union Law creates with our own British ideals, principles and doctrines both constitutionally and in terms of liberty or freedom, we can examine the more relevant parts. You will find them to be quite intriguing.

Article 2 of the TOEU claims that the European Union is:

> *"...founded on the values of respect for human dignity, freedom, democracy, equality, the rule of law and respect for human rights, including the rights of persons belonging to minorities* [49]*."*

Again, the words contained in this codified legal document are immensely ambiguous; a somewhat recurring theme in European Law, and one that I suspect is intentional to as to level out a broad field for those in control to play out their own plans to the advantage of themselves and the indifference of those beneath them. Words like *"pluralism"*, *"tolerance"*, *"non-discrimination"*, *"justice"*, *"solidarity"* and *"equality"* are all put to good use in the empty poetry of Article 2 of this treaty. It is not particularly necessary for me to point out the obvious, but I shall do so in any case. These words, at least when taken outside of any real context such as they are in this Article, are empty. Article 2 also states:

---

[49] Article G, *Treaty on European Union* OJ C 191, 29.7.1992, p. 1–112

"The Community shall have as its task, by establishing a common market and an economic and monetary union and by implementing the common policies or activities referred to in Articles 3 and 3a, to promote throughout the Community a harmonious and balanced development of economic activities, sustainable and non-inflationary growth respecting the environment, a high degree of convergence of economic performance, a high level of employment and of social protection, the raising of the standard of living and quality of life, and economic and social cohesion and solidarity among Member States [50]."

Of course, it goes without saying that for those small minded individuals who refuse to think critically and are easily swayed by buzzwords and emotiveness, that simply including these pieces of key vocabulary is sufficient and any action to the contrary is subsequently ignored. Nevertheless, they are unlikely to be enough for any individual who cares about truth and liberty; one who thinks critically and deeply and seeks clarification on the reality of the world as opposed to crafting a world within their own reality. What is equality? What does the European Union mean by justice? Is multiculturalism the same as pluralism? If the European Union adores pluralism so much then why are they so insistent on destroying member state's cultures and homogenising them into a faux-culture manifest in an entirely manufactured *'European'* identity?

The Maastricht Treaty was responsible for the introduction of the Monetary Union that we see wreaking havoc today on the lives of millions of people across Europe. The Eurozone Crisis (the Eurozone being those countries that

---

[50] ^Ibid

are part of the Euro) has been continuing since 2009 and does not realistically show any sign of going away. Countries such as Greece, Spain, Ireland and Portugal have all been plunged into an abyss of debt, reliance and misery. How did this happen? Well it is of course a complicated affair, but the basic outline is still nonetheless comprehensible.

The Maastricht Treaty created a monetary union, which meant one single currency and one single central bank for all of the member states in the Eurozone. In International Financial Law, most countries are given a credit rating, which is decided by the an international credit ratings agency, the two biggest being *Moody's Investment Service* and *Standard and Poor.* These agencies grant countries a credit rating, which just as with an individual, influence the borrowing terms, interest rates, etc. of a nation. Consequently, a poorer country with higher debt will have a more negative credit rating, and thus a lower borrowing limit and a higher interest rate, compared with a country that has a good credit rating and thus can borrow more at lower rates. When the monetary union was introduced, and smaller or poorer countries joined, the economies were essentially compiled into one giant economy despite being extremely different. The result of this is that the European Union is considered as one when member states are borrowing, which in turn creates a false idea of the ability of a country to repay its debts. In other words, poorer countries such as Greece, are able to borrow at a higher rate than they would ordinarily be allowed to, and at lower interest rates, despite not potentially having the ability to repay the debts.

The rise in consumer borrowing across Europe, as a result

of irresponsible lending and borrowing, meant that eventually, when individuals defaulted on their debts, the banks were unable to repay theirs. This was one of the reasons we saw a financial crisis, which resulted in member state governments needing to borrow in order to bail the banks out. However, the bailouts that the banks received from the European Union in countries such as Spain, which went via the government, turned what was a financial crisis into a monetary crisis, which had a direct impact on the entire economy of the Eurozone. Which continues to shrink again to this day

The United Kingdom thankfully managed to opt out of joining the Euro, which meant that we were not hit as hard as the Eurozone was. However, this didn't mean that we escaped altogether, the United Kingdom's markets were inevitably affected and the United Kingdom itself was ordered to contribute towards the Eurozone bailout.

This has a direct impact on the individual, because of course, the more the United Kingdom has to bail out other, irresponsible nations for being part of a program that the United Kingdom turned down, the more you have to pay in your taxes. The individual suffers in a number of ways, in that their own money is used to pay the bailout, and is not spent on vital services, infrastructure and investment. Surely, it would be better, if the billions that the United Kingdom has paid to the European Union in bailouts and contributions were spent on our own country, whilst trade deals were sought with the hundreds of nations across the globe?

If the monetary union created by the Maastricht Treaty were not convincing enough, take the example of Cyprus. Here we see an example where the European Union really does trample on the liberties of the individual. When Cyprus had a similar situation to Greece, Spain, Ireland and Portugal, the European Union actually raided the bank accounts of civilians, rich and poor, living there. This included British citizens. In English law, private business is immensely important, and so your bank account is a private matter between you and your bank, who owe you a whole host of duties under the law. In essence, the United Kingdom government would never in a million years be able to raid your bank account without some due process of law. Yet the European Union strolled in and took a levy from the savings account of every single person with savings in Cyprus. This is the epitome of a dictatorial regime that not only feels it can place itself above the courts, the law and liberties, but thinks it can help itself to your savings and bank balance too.

In the Greek situation, an offer was made to Greece that essentially made Germany and other member states, as well as the European Union, the owners of Greece. It did so by forcing the hand over of ports, landmarks and other assets in return for the bailout loan. The terms were so oppressive and contemptuous of democracy, sovereignty and basic liberties, that the Greeks held a referendum on whether to accept them. The response from the Greek people comprised of a resounding no, not that this mattered at all. The Greek Government were forced in any case, to accept the terms, and the overthrowing of the democratic will of the populous soiled the home of the original democracy.

For a treaty that has direct effect, and therefore is supposed to confer rights on citizens and obligations on governments; for a treaty that claims to uphold the values of human dignity or freedom; for a treaty that supposedly implements measure that are supposed to encourage economic growth and high performing economies; for a treaty that is supposed to create a 'community'; it really does not live up to its purpose. It has destroyed economies, removed sovereignty, overthrown democracy to the extent that it matters not which party governs because they act as a puppet, trampled on human dignity and created the division and impossibility of any real community. It is abhorrent, and there is nothing that we can do about it, unless we choose to leave.

The Treaty of Rome (TFFOEU)

The Treaty for the Functioning of the European Union (TFFOEU), or alternatively the Treaty of Rome, is a landmark treaty that carries with it several implications. Many of you will have heard of the Treaty of Rome, or at least heard it mentioned in debates, news reports, interviews and so forth. This is because it is perhaps the most relevant Treaty of our time concerning the European Union. The Treaty of Rome contains numerous extremely significant elements, with some are more relevant to Britain, at least in a direct sense, than others. It is Treaty of Rome that regulates the European Union internal market; introduces the Euro, which was by all accounts a failure —an intended one I suspect, designed to entrap poorer nations and commit wealthier ones; it covers the free movement of goods, services, capital and people; it governs the cooperation and elements of operation concerning justice, security and the police forces of member states; it covers transport; competition legislation in business and finance; industry, the environment, taxation, employment, social policy, industry, energy, etc. The list is quite frankly endless. The almost exhaustive nature of the Treaty has a rather specific, clear and straightforward explanation for it, which we will come to later.

Article 34 of the Treaty for the Functioning of the European Union sought to create a pan-European common market[51], which was intended to expand European trade and open up the EU market to free trade amongst the various member states. In principle, this idea is a noble one; anything, which permits and enables free trading amongst various countries in a global economy, should be applauded for their competitive spirit and their wise approach. Indeed, freedom to trade, I would argue, is another liberty that applies to the individual as much as it does to the nation. Free trade should be regarded in essence as the freedom of the individual, or in this case the freedom of a nation, to go about its own private business unhindered, for the benefit of those party to any trade relationships. English law has long held private business to be a fundamentally important right, which is best manifest in contract law.

Nevertheless, whilst the principle of opening up free trade in Europe is easily justified, it can still be said that with the modern state of affairs there is a tremendous overreach of power that has been transferred. The Courts of Justice have interpreted Article 34 in such a way that emphasis is placed so much on the restriction of domestic nations with regards to marketing their own products, so much so that the article has been taken to apply to broadly when restricting these rights, and not broadly enough when empowering domestic nations. The end result of this is quite simply that

---

[51] Article 34, *Treaty on the Functioning of the European Union* OJ C 326, 26.10.2012, p. 47–390

in an attempt to open up a free pan-European common market, the Courts of Justice have in fact restricted it. The truth of this matter will be discovered upon elaboration, however there is an immensely strong argument that the European Courts have placed such a broad meaning on the prohibitions in Article 34 that it leaves no room for domestic nation-state regulation and policy-making.

Article 34 more specifically concerns the non-fiscal barriers of quotas and measures having equivalent effect. The prohibition that is mentioned in the question concerns non-fiscal measures, namely the prohibition in Article 34 of quantitative restrictions and measures having equal effect. Article 34 states that *"Quantitative restrictions on imports and all measures having equivalent effect shall be prohibited between Member States[52]"*. This simply means that Member States are forbidden from imposing any kinds of restrictions on the number, or quantity, on goods. You will remember from our previous mention of how civil codes work, that with the European Union law working on a civil code, the wording of the article is vitally important. Evidently, the wording of this particular article creates an enormously broad concept, given that it essentially bans specific quantitative restrictions, but also any measure that carries with it the same result as a quantitative restriction. In fact, the meaning of this is found in the case of *Geddo v Ente Nazionale Rizi*, where it was held that the words of Article 34 meant *"... a total or partial restraint of... imports, exports or goods in transit [53]."*

Quantitative restrictions can be separated into two different

---

[52] ^Ibid
[53] GEDDO -V- ENTE NAZIONALE RISI; ECJ 12 JUL 1973

types. One such type is any type of restriction on the quantity of imported goods, as found in the case of *R v Henn and Darby*[54], the other is any kind of quotas set down on imported goods as is found in the case of International Fruit Company (No2).   Moreover, a 'Measure Having Equivalent Effect' (MEQR) derives from two sources of law; one is the definition in the case of *Procureur du Roi v Dassonville*, where it was held that

> *"All trading rules enacted by Member States which are capable of hindering, directly or indirectly, actually or potentially, intra-Community trade are to be considered as measures having equivalent effect to quantitative restrictions* [55]*".*

Furthermore the other source is Directive 70/50 which separates measures having equivalent effect into two types; Article 2 concerns distinctly applicable MEQRs, which are measures that do not apply equally to domestic and imported goods, and Article 3 concerns indistinctly applicable MEQRs which are measures that do not apply equally to domestic and imported goods[56]. One issue that can immediately be raised regarding the definition given in the Dassonville case is that again, in the true fashion of European Union law, the interpretation is far too broad. Peter Oliver, former law clerk to the past Advocate General of the European Courts of Justice, states in his essay in the Fordham International Law Journal that:

> *"The striking feature of the Dassonville formula is its breadth. In particular, it is not necessary to show that a*

---

[54] Regina v. Henn. &. Darby. 34/79, ECJ

[55] Procureur du Roi v Benoît and Gustave Dassonville (1974) Case 8/74

[56] Directive 70/50/EEC of 22 December 1969 OJ L 13, 19.1.1970, p. 29–31

> *measure actually restricts imports, but only that it potentially does so...[57]"*

Accordingly, whilst the article was initially concerned with the general rules of trade, it is clear from subsequent cases that the definition given in the Dassonville case had widened the scope dramatically enough to allow the Court to make various preceding rulings that arguably went further than mere trading rules. For example, in the case of Commission v Ireland, or the 'Buy Irish Case', and the Commission v Ireland 'Irish Souvenirs Case', a breach was found in relation to the Irish government promoting Irish products. Moreover, in the case of *Firma Denkavit* inspections were also found to be in breach[58]. These cases obviously involved domestic governments taking clear protective measures, and the Dassonville formula exterminating these measures, often without regard for the reason behind them. Consequently, the European Courts of Justice were not interested in what the reason for any measure was, but simply that a measure had been taken, and whether this measure could 'potentially' breach the Article rather than whether it actually had. Since the Dassonville's formula focused on the measures themselves rather than the reason for the measures, it established a broad principle that was perhaps too restrictive for domestic governments. In fact, a series of cases known as *'The Sunday Trading cases'* demonstrated that post Dassonville there was a sort of precedent laid down that meant the European Courts could easily stamp out any national governments actions that they deemed to stand in

---

[57] Oliver, Peter; *'Of Trailer and Jet Skis: Is the Case Law on Article 34 TFEU Hurtling in a New Direction?'*, p.7, Fordham International Law Journal, Volume 33, Issue 15, Article 4, 2011.

[58] Firma Denkavit Futtermittel GmbH v Minister für Ernähung, Landwirtschaft und Forsten des Landes Nordrhein-Westfalen. Case 251/78.

the way of 'free trade', or at least the European Union's idea of it.

Consequently, in 1978, the scope of the formula was reduced in the case of *Cassis de Dijon*[59]. This essentially elaborated on the idea of distinctly and indistinctly applicable measures having equivalent effect; the case involved the German regulations requiring certain types of alcohol to be above 25% in alcohol content in order to be sold on the German market. The court found that this measure was indistinctly applicable because the intention of the German government was not to ban the import of foreign alcoholic beverages, but had an effect on imported goods, despite not being aimed solely at them. Due to this reasoning of distinct and indistinct applicability, some may argue that the scope of powers that were technically restricted by the Dassonville interpretation of Article 34, were now extended to allow domestic governments the power to impose measures provided that they satisfied certain obligatory criteria. These 'mandatory requirements' laid out in the Cassis case, meant that such measures could be justified if they were in place for effectiveness of fiscal supervision, the protection of public health, the fairness of commercial transactions and the defence of the consumer. Aside from the mandatory requirements that came out of Cassis, so too did the *'Presumption of Mutuality'*, which meant that if the regulatory requirements for a product were met in one Member States, they were met in all Member States[60]. These principles laid out in Cassis, applied only to indistinctly applicable MEQRs only. In one sense, this

---

[59] Rewe-Zentral AG v Bundesmonopolverwaltung für Branntwein (1979) Case 120/78

[60] ^Ibid

interpretation by the Courts contradicts the original point made regarding the interpretation on the prohibition being too wide, and the interpretation on national sovereignty over markets and policies being too narrow, since it essentially grants extra powers to domestic governments to enable them to introduce certain measures. Whilst some may argue that Cassis is narrowing the rule originally found in Dassonville, what it does do is grant some leniency to domestic nations to introduce, in controlled circumstances, some measures that may ordinarily be in breach of Article 34 of the Treaty for the Functioning of the European Union. However, the original question is not one of some freedom for domestic governments, it is one of the imbalance between the interpretation of the prohibition and the interpretation of the freedom of domestic nations ; essentially trade sovereignty.

The European Courts of Justice's interpretation, essentially outlawed under EU Law, any national campaign to promote domestic products, because it may well result in *"Hindering...intra-community trade...*[61]*"* A criticism of this would be that, just as the original question states, it in fact restricts a domestic governments ability to make policies and market its products. This could result, not in leveling the playing field, but rather in stifling any healthy competition between products from different nations by eliminating domestic governments' ability to compete and centralising control of trade to the European Union in its entirety. Daniel Hannan, Conservative Eurosceptic Member of the European Parliament, wrote;

"...every continent on the planet is now experiencing economic

---

[61] Cassis de Dijon judgement (CJ Case 120/78, 20 February 1979)

growth except Europe. Individual EU states can't sign bilateral free-trade agreements with, say, China or India; they have to wait for Brussels to do so on their behalf. For a country as naturally inclined to open commerce as Britain, this is a real disadvantage, since we are in effect dragged into a protectionist common position[62]".

It is interesting to note that the Courts' interpretation of Article 34 was apparently about eliminating protectionism and leveling the playing field, however Daniel Hannan points out that the EU has actually become protectionist itself with regards to its global relationship. Consequently, is Article 34 about protecting Europe from protectionism, or is it about stifling national sovereignty over trade, and transferring it to the EU in place of nation-states? I would suspect, on balance, that it is in fact the latter.

One developmental case to pay attention to with regards to Article 34 is the *Keck Case*, out of which came the *'Keck test'*, which sought to expand on Dassonville[63]. Some academics such as Stephen Weatherill claimed the European Court had *"...changed its mind[64]"*, however the official position was that the Dassonville formula in terms of not hindering trade, was still standing. What the Keck test did do however was form a further distinction between indistinctly applicable MEQRs and selling arrangements. As a result, the Court was essentially saying that if a measure satisfied the Keck test, it was not an MEQR, and therefore it could

---

[62] Hannan, Daniel; Conservative Home: *'Nine myths about the EU'*, 7th January 2015, Retrieved 3rd March 2016 -
http://www.conservativehome.com/thecolumnists/2015/01/daniel-hannan-mep-nine-myths-about-the-eu.html
[63] Joined Cases C-267/91 and C-268/91 Keck and Mithouard [1993] ECR I-6097.
[64] Stephen Weatherill, *Cases and Materials on EU Law* (10th Edition, 2012, OUP) [328]

be justified. The requirements that came out of Keck to form the 'Keck Test' were; that the measures apply to all relevant traders within the national territory, and that the measures have the same impact in both law and fact, on both domestic and imported products. This obviously represents a dramatic shift in that it appears, at least in principle, that the Court is effectively moving away from its previous position of almost rendering national government impotent with regards to their own trading arrangements, and into a more open approach that gave governments freedom to introduce measures based on the impact. As mentioned previously, the Dassonville case resulted in the Courts being interested in the measure that had been taken, irrespective of the outcome of that measure, since it only needed to be a potential hindrance. Whilst the ruling in Keck was with absolute regard for the result and intention of the measure, which some may say is a more pragmatic approach but nonetheless a contradiction of the Dassonville formula.

The Keck case can is argued by some to be the granting of more freedoms to member states to introduce measures. The introduction of the Keck test, in the opinion of some was a limit on European Law rather than on nation states, and in fact promoted greater social rights; Miguel Maduro, Portuguese academic and politician, claimed that

> "*The limits set in Keck to challenges... to national rules the effect of which is to limit the commercial freedom of traders, will reduce the impact of the free movement of goods on national legislation protecting social rights* [65]".

---

[65] Shaw, Jo; '*Social Law and Policy in an Evolving European Union*', p.334, Bloomsbury Publishing, 18th December 2000.

Here he implies that prior to Keck, the interpretations of the courts limited commercial freedom, and that Keck in fact gave some of that freedom back. However, it is almost an admission from the former Advocate General, that the general interpretation was stifling national legislation, which could be viewed by some as an intrusion on sovereignty such as the type mentioned in the initial question.

Aside from an Article 36 derogation, or meeting the mandatory requirements set out in Cassis de Dijon, the Keck test is the only way that an MEQR can be excluded from the scrutiny of Article 34. This evidently still shows a somewhat strict attitude from the European Courts on trading, since even selling arrangements restrict competition to some extent by ensuring the arrangements are applied to all goods whether they are imported or not. Advocate General Jacobs stated that, in his view, the one principle of Article 34 was that

> *"all undertakings which engage in a legitimate economic activity in a Member State should have unfettered access to the whole of the Community market [66] ".*

Nevertheless, is this not still rather broad? Since the effect of the Courts' interpretation of Article 34 is to limit the national legislation, which makes the word 'legitimate' a somewhat loosely defined one. Legitimate according to whom? Advocate General Jacobs went on to say

> *"Once it is recognized that there is a need to limit the scope of Article 30 (now Art 34 TFEU) in order to prevent excessive*

---

[66] Opinion of Mr. Advocate General Jacobs delivered on 24 November 1994. Case C-412/93.

interference in the regulatory powers of the Member States, a test based on the extent to which a measure hinders trade between Member States by restricting market access seems the most obvious solution [67]".

It seems that Jacobs submits that the Courts' interpretations are interfering too much with the member states, and that this should be curtailed, which might suggest he shares some agreement with the initial comment.

Another criticism that can be given to the Keck test is also that there are certain arrangements that do not fit into any category. Advertising for example, cannot fit into any of the two categories and so the scope, whilst broad in terms of its restrictions in national powers, is not broad enough to cover all situations. Nevertheless, some argue that the Keck test is still a success and has stood the test of time so far. For example Dr. Felicitas Parapatits wrote;

> *"Although the distinction has its shortcomings, especially because certain measures, such as advertisement regulations, cannot be put in one of the two categories, the Court has continually and successfully applied the Keck framework until today[68]."*

Consequently, whilst the Keck test has enabled Article 34 to become clearer and more flexible than it had been the past, it is still ultimately restrictive in practice; it seem restriction is something the European Union consistently demonstrates an obsession with. Not necessarily because it

---

[67] ^Ibid

[68] Parapatits, Felicitas Dr.; *'The Influence of the (post) Keck Case Law on the Freedom to Provide Services'*, (No Date Given), (PDF Format: http://www.stiftung.at/wp-content/uploads/2012/06/The_Influence_of_the_post_Keck_Case_Law_on_the_Freedom_to_Provide_Services-Felicitas-Parapatits.pdf).

places extra regulations, but rather that the mixture of various rulings in various cases appear to be complicated without good reason. Essentially, the courts have a series of cases whereby every kind of slight domestic regulation can be overturned without the approval of the European Court, whilst at the same time allowed. One would argue that the result of this is not freedom of movement of goods, but rather the dormant power of the European Courts to act as market regulators, by classifying certain types of transactions however they wish to, in order to achieve a certain result. This does not necessarily *always* happen, but the whether it does, or it doesn't, the potential is there, and so eventually it will happen.

Additionally, due to the confused manner in which the Court has inconsistently applied its judgments, it isn't simply a matter of interpretation too broadly, but rather not interpreting clearly, resulting in a tortuous conclusion that nobody can be completely sure of. I believe that logic and reason, in light of our increased awareness of, and experience with, the working of the European Union and its legal system, indicates this to be intentional. It is for all intents and purposes, to grant greater fluidity to the court to regulate, however the more the court regulates, the less the member state may do so, and the result of this is that more definitions and rulings appear to broaden the scope of Article 34 by making it more codified and more rigid in its implementation, turning the common market into a less competitive, centralised one.

What this tells us, is that the European Union is not about trade or freedom, it is about restriction, power and expansion. You will see how the European Courts not only overreach their authority, but do so by twisting and manipulating the law, and bringing in absurd tests and conventions without any basis, in order to use the law always to the advantage of the European project. If the European Union is willing to do this to businesses, they are willing to do it to individuals too.

In fact, there is a direct evidence of this. In October 2004, the European Union introduced *the Treaty establishing a Constitution for Europe*. This Treaty almost came into being, but was rejected eventually. It sought to impose a constitution on member states, which would override domestic constitutions including our own. Naturally the supremacy of EU law and the methods by which European Union laws are enforced already does in many ways, but a European Union Constitution would have cemented the whole process, since a constitution was the one element missing to finally make the European Union into a super-state. Both the French and the Dutch rejected, quite rightly, this dangerous and repulsive document outright, via referenda. In a functioning democracy of course, that should be the end of it. It wasn't.

Instead, the treaty was amended slightly, albeit in frivolous areas, and subsequently repackaged as the *Treaty of Lisbon*. This treaty amended the two aforementioned treaties *(Maastricht & Rome)* in a way that essentially brought the rejected *Treaty establishing a Constitution for Europe* into effect by the back door.

The result? The European Union has a constitution by proxy, and is in all but name a super-state which little care for the democratic will of nations or people. The Lisbon Treaty is simply the European Constitution, and our own glorious constitution has been reduced to a museum piece despite the immense power and freedom it grants you as an individual. If you care for your own individual liberty and the rights of people to run their own lives, then you will view the Lisbon Treaty and those treaties that it brings together, with nothing but the contempt that they deserve. Regardless of how you feel though, these treaties, by virtue of the Lisbon Treaty along with the doctrine of direct effect, are your Gods now. Unless of course, when the time comes, you decide to say 'no'.

CHAPTER 8
BYPASSING DEMOCRACY

Direct applicability is often confused with Direct Effect but the two are actually different. Direct applicability concerns those pieces of law that do not require any action on the part of the domestic governments, parliaments or other institutions, in order for those said pieces of legislation to come into effect in the respective nations. Essentially, in layman's terms, direct applicability simply means that the European Union's Council of Ministers enact law directly into member states; there is no need to tell the member states to do anything, because where directly applicable legislation is concerned, domestic, democratically elected governments, are wholly irrelevant.

Some might argue that this isn't a completely undemocratic method. After all, the Council of Ministers, or what is otherwise known as the Council of the European Union, is composed of Ministers from the member states who convene together to enact intergovernmental legislation across the European Union. Consequently, it is the opinion of pro-EU advocates that there is a justification for the Council having a further reaching arm than the European Parliament in terms of legislation that is meant to be coordinated across the various member states. Since the Council is made up of government ministers from those states who have been elected, they arguably have a democratic mandate to pass the laws that they do.

This is of course, in keeping with the pro-EU culture, vehemently misleading. Whilst the Council is made up of democratically elected officials, the laws that they produce are applicable directly in each of their member states despite the fact they have been created by a group that consists of only one elected official from that member state. In the case of the United Kingdom this is particularly questionable because of the fact that the Minister who is representing the United Kingdom at the meeting would not ordinarily be able to pass such legislation on their own within their own nation.

Allow me to elaborate in order to give some greater clarification on this. The Home Secretary Theresa May submitted a Bill to Parliament titled *The Draft Communications Data Bill*. It proposed that Internet and mobile phone companies should be required, by law, to collect, retain and maintain information on the activity of those members of the public using their services. The draft legislation details that this would include social media, emails, phone calls, games, any kind of messaging facilities, and more; requiring that this information be stored for a year[69]. Proponents of the Bill claimed that it was necessary for reasons of national security, whilst opponents condemned it as the Government essentially trying to spy on its citizens; labelling it the 'Snooper's Charter'.

---

[69] Draft Communications Data Bill 2012:
https://www.gov.uk/government/uploads/system/uploads/attachment_data/file/228824/8359.pdf

Focusing on this Bill for just one moment, I would suggest that there are two major problems with it. Firstly, it is ultimately quite vague in nature, which is a common and yet dangerous aspect of any law that is supposed to be there to protect 'security'. If a Bill is too vague then it opens itself up to wider interpretation and this grants much broader powers to authorities over the individual than the public might ultimately suspect —essentially it is misleading and deceitful.

However the greater problem with it; is that it undermines a serious and important principle of English law, one that like many others was first pioneered by England and which the world now takes for granted. This is the principle of being innocent until proven guilty. Every individual should be treated as innocent until they are proven guilty, and this must ultimately extend to restricting the state or an individual's neighbour from delving into their private affairs 'just in case' that individual has done something wrong. To demand that by law that companies have to spy on their own customers, not only interferes with private enterprise in a way that verges on totalitarian, it also supposes that anyone who might object to it may have something to hide. If a government is checking, directly or indirectly, just in case someone, somewhere, might be doing something wrong, then they are not policing but rather they are snooping; which intrinsically undermines the presumption of innocence that is so immensely vital to English law, liberties and democracy. With that in mind, the term 'Snooper's Charter' is not a caricature or a mockery; it is an absolutely accurate and indeed far more honest title for this deeply concerning piece of draft legislation.

It is only by virtue of the United Kingdom's constitutional structure, and in particular Parliamentary Supremacy with its three elements, that prevents this legislation from being simply and easily forced onto the people of the United Kingdom. In order for the legislation to pass, it must of course go through the required procedures or readings in both the House of Commons and House of Lords, before then being signed into law by Her Majesty. In essence, as is reasonably clear to most people, it is extremely difficult for the Government, or even the House of Commons –let alone Theresa May alone, to impose this law onto us all at will. This is quite simply because it is not the Government who are sovereign or supreme, nor is it the House of Commons or any individual Minister; Parliament in its complete form is supreme and sovereign, and so if one element is missing, the Bill will not pass. This is an important safeguard for all of those, including those who sit on the benches in Parliament, who have to live with the consequences of laws.

Remember, as much as it may not seem to always be the case, politicians must also live under the law that they help to create, so by having the different separation of duties and powers in Parliament and investing sovereignty in no single individual but rather in Parliament as a collective, it provides the nation with reasonable safeguards against the tyranny of one single person who is not accountable for their actions nor subject to the laws that they directly create. This is one of the reasons why wars were fought and people were killed in order to create our Parliamentary Democracy, under the constitution that we have since enjoyed the benefits of and which has since been copied numerous times over globally. The system, structure and constitution were put in place exactly for this reason and others. Thus, owing to the very sensible system that the United Kingdom employs, which separates sovereignty or supremacy out so that it is dispersed in different ways or forms amongst numerous bodies, in order to protect us from any despotism. Ministers alone cannot make law and implement law, so there are many hoops for Theresa May and her fellow snoopers to jump through before they can get this kind of legislation passed through Parliament.

Nevertheless, for the sake of illustrating an important principle and point, I ask that you imagine for a moment that no such system were in place. Imagine if for a moment, rather than needing to jump through the aforementioned hoops in order to get the law passed, Theresa May was instead able to convene with a number of random individuals from other organisations or governments, decide on an agenda, do a few favours, and upon reaching an agreement to pass the law, walk out of the meeting with the power to start browsing your text messages and internet history. Imagine how simple and easy it would be for Theresa May to circumvent Parliament if this were possible, and in doing so circumvent all of the protections that Parliament's system gives us; any democratic mandates granted by the public; or any apparent manifesto pledges. It would undoubtedly make life exceptionally easy for Theresa May or any other respective Minister who wished to do the same. It would also create an exceptionally easy method by which laws can be enacted without all that inconvenient nonsense about scrutiny, amendments or accountability. It would also all but dismantle Parliament's very purpose, thus bringing into question the need at all for a Parliament.

Consider then for a moment, this sort of situation. Is it not a horrendous insult to the principles that have created one of the greatest governmental structures the world has ever seen? Is it not akin to trampling on the graves of those who died valiantly in order to create, protect and pass it on to us? Is it not, ultimately, an affront to the very concept of democracy? Indeed it is. Yet horrifically, this is exactly what direct applicability does. Whilst it is correct that each country democratically elects the Minister representing them, in some form or other, it is neither correct nor logical to deduct that by virtue of this, the Council and their directly applicable laws are somehow automatically democratic. Why is it not democratic? Well the reasons are two fold; firstly, whilst the representative of each nation is elected by that nation, they are not elected by the other nations involved. In other words the majority of the influence comes from individuals elected by foreign nations, and thus individuals who are essentially the practical equivalent of unelected people in relation to the United Kingdom. Certainly this works in reverse too, in that each country is essentially a minority, but I would maintain that this is merely the sign of a further flaw rather than a positive aspect.

Just because a group of people must potentially compromise on absolutely everything in order to reach a decision, doesn't mean that this group is a democratic or accountable group. The point is that in these instances, it is not the British people holding their representative to account through the medium of elected representatives that reflect a cross-section of views; rather, it is a number of foreign leaders holding our own to account. This places all of the checks, balances and accountability into the wrong hands, which ultimately results in an allegiance on the part of our own politicians to the agenda driven by the trends of European countries.

Consequently, it is of course no wonder that people are sceptical about the line of argument that some pro-EU figures are using; that Britain must remain in the European Union in order to have an influence over legislation. In the period 2009 – 2015, the United Kingdom was outvoted on 12.3% of occasions on the European Council[70]. This may seem to be a relatively small percentage in relation to 100%, however in relation to other EU nations it is not. Aside from Britain, the other two largest member states in the European Union and thus on the European Council are France and Germany. In the same period that the United Kingdom was outvoted 12.3% of the time, France was on the losing side less than 2% of the time and Germany was on the losing side less than 6% of the time[71]. This means that essentially the United Kingdom was outvoted on the European Council 6 times more than France and twice as much as Germany. I am unsure what others may think, but by my own estimations that does not give the United Kingdom a glowing report in terms of influence.

On top of this lack of influence, it is important to note another element that further brings into question just how

[70] Hix, Simon; Hagemann, Sara; & Frantescu, Doru; *Would Brexit Matter? The UK's Voting Record in the Council and European Parliament*, VoteWatch.eu, Brussels, 19 April 2016 (PDF Format: http://60811b39eee4e42e277a-72b421883bb5b133f34e068afdd7cb11.r29.cf3.rackcdn.com/2016/04/VoteWatch-Report-2016_digital.pdf)

[71] Hix, Simon; Hagemann, Sara; & Frantescu, Doru; *Would Brexit Matter? The UK's Voting Record in the Council and European Parliament*, VoteWatch.eu, Brussels, 19 April 2016 (PDF Format: http://60811b39eee4e42e277a-72b421883bb5b133f34e068afdd7cb11.r29.cf3.rackcdn.com/2016/04/VoteWatch-Report-2016_digital.pdf)

democratic and accountable the European Council, and direct applicability is. The EU Parliament, and the European Commission, both have a vote on the European Council in the same way that national governments do. Naturally the EU Parliament is given a vote because the people of Europe have elected the people who populate its soulless chambers. After all, the European Union cares deeply for you all, and wants your voices to be heard. I am of course being sarcastic when I say this, because in actuality it is nothing more than the sprinkling of electoral crumbs from a towering table to the peasants wailing and crying below –us.

Alas, it is quite clear that the United Kingdom has very little influence on the Council of Ministers and therefore really doesn't hold much power in legislative matters concerning direct applicability. Nevertheless, what of the influence held by the United Kingdom in the European Parliament; principally the only element of the EU legislature that is directly elected by the citizens of the members states? According to the Brussels based group; VoteWatch.eu, the figures don't especially do much to instil any greater confidence in this area either. In the period 2009 – 2015, the United Kingdom MEPs were more likely than ever before to be outvoted, and more likely than their colleagues from other member states. The report by VoteWatch.eu states:

> " *Overall, European Parliament voting records suggest that the UK is in a weak position in this branch of the EU's legislative system. Most British MEPs do not sit in the groups that dominate the European Parliament agenda. And even when they do sit in these groups – such as the Conservatives in EPP before 2009, and Labour in S&D – British MEPs*

are often opposed to the majority positions of these groups. As a result, British MEPs often find themselves on the losing side in key votes [72]."

Not only does the United Kingdom have very little influence on the European Council, but it also has a relatively low influence in the European Parliament. This allows the other member states, or at least those who conform to the fashionable agenda of the day, to dominate the already questionable 'democratic' proceedings, and in doing so impose the conclusions, in many cases, via direct applicability on every single member state regardless of their position, and irrespective of the opinion of their national Parliaments —who are circumvented. So the question remains; if we are to remain in the United Kingdom to exercise influence over the decisions and laws that are made, then how can we exercise said influence from a position of marginalisation and minority voting?

Well, there is an answer to this of course. One simple answer that should already be quite apparent in light of what has been discussed. The answer lies in what I would assert, based on the information, may well be the very reason for the design of this imbalanced and faux-democratic system. The answer is a contradictory and paradoxical one; if the United Kingdom wishes to exert more influence over the agenda, decisions, direction and laws passed in the European Union, they must learn to agree with the European Union's agenda, decisions,

---

[72] Hix, Simon; Hagemann, Sara; & Frantescu, Doru; *'Would Brexit Matter? The UK's Voting Record in the Council and European Parliament'*, p.8, VoteWatch.eu, Brussels, 19 April 2016 (PDF Format: http://60811b39eee4e42e277a-72b421883bb5b133f34e068afdd7cb11.r29.cf3.rackcdn.com/2016/04/VoteWatch-Report-2016_digital.pdf)

direction and laws of the European Union. Undeniably, there is no other way for the United Kingdom to be on the winning side in the European Union Parliament or the Council of Ministers, other than to comply even against its own better judgment.

I am sure it is quite obvious, that whilst this is not a satirical answer but rather a realistic and honest one, it is nevertheless a contradiction by its very nature. It is another way of saying that the United Kingdom has no influence, and if it wants any influence, it must cease to have any desire to have any influence. The United Kingdom must stop wanting what the European Union does not wish to give it. In short, it is impossible for the United Kingdom to have any influence, so the only option is for the United Kingdom, just as the European Union does with its democratic processes, to simply create the illusion that it has influence and hope that its people never really notice.

CHAPTER 9
JUST FOLLOWING ORDERS

It was the case of *Van Gend En Loos*, which concerned customs duties that were being placed on goods imported from another member state, which first created the doctrine of direct effect[73]. In this case the courts declared that because of direct effect, the duties were contrary to Article 12 of the EEC Treaty. The doctrine of direct effect for which Van Gend En Loos became the founding case, concerns situations where a law is enacted in a member state 'directly' from the European Union in a way that grants or bestows rights on EU citizens, or citizens of member states to bring claims in court their own domestic courts[74]. In the case of Van Gend en Loos, it was ruled that the articles of European Union treaties create rights for individuals, which domestic or national courts are obliged to protect[75].

There are two forms which direct effect takes: vertical and horizontal. This is an incredibly complicated and confusing

---

[73] Craig, Paul; de Búrca, Gráinne (2003). *EU Law: Text, Cases and Materials* (3rd ed.). p. 182, Oxford University Press.

[74] *Van Gend en Loos v Nederlandse Administratie der Belastingen* (1963) Case 26/62

[75] *Van Gend en Loos v Nederlandse Administratie der Belastingen* (1963) Case 26/62

area of European Law, however I will try to explain it as simply as possible. Both situations concern European Union law that has direct effect; vertical direct effect concerns those situations between European Union law and domestic law which by placing obligations on the state to adhere to the law, it confer rights on citizens to bring action against the state or public bodies under European Union law. Note that the expression used in *Foster v. British Gas plc.* the landmark case on this, is any body that is an *"emanation of the state*[76]*"*, so this can also include private bodies that are performing functions of the state and various other public bodies. Horizontal direct effect is where European Law is able to be used between private bodies, be they individual or company, against each other rather than against the state.

Whether a piece of European Union law has direct effect, depends on the form that it takes. As we already know from *Van Gend en Loos*, articles in treaties do have direct effect, and indeed they are also directly applicable because the domestic government does not need to do anything to bring them into domestic law (something we will tough on more later). Regulations are another form of European Union law that has direct effect. The basis for granting direct effect to regulations, can be found in Article 288 in the Treaty for the Function of the European Union, which states that; *"A regulation shall have general application. It shall be binding in its entirety and directly applicable in all Member States*[77]*."* This is should concern you, since regulations are essentially the European Union's version of Acts of Parliament, and

---

[76] *Foster v British Gas plc* (1990) C-188/89

[77] *Treaty on the Functioning of the European Union [2007]*, OJ C 326, Chapter 2, Section 1, Article 288.

gives the same effect over member states. Regulations are both directly applicable and directly effective, and the European Commission, which is made up of unelected bureaucrats you have never heard of, can have the ability to make regulations delegated to them from the Council of Ministers[78]. This essentially grants the Commission an immense amount of power, whilst granting you absolutely no power to remove or hold them to account. Regulations are ultimately the most authoritative tool that the European Union has in order to make law that governs are lives. The binding nature and the unaccountable manner, in which they can be passed, shall be covered as easily as possible in the following chapter on *Direct Applicability*.

Contrasting with this, is *indirect effect*, which in any other situation or case will apply. Indirect effect comes into play when direct effect has either failed or does not apply; this forces domestic governments to interpret their own domestic law in line with European Union law.

So for example, imagine that a Directive is introduced that bestows an obligation on the United Kingdom to ensure that it becomes law that all kittens are murdered, and they demand that this law be in place by 2020, but there is an Act of Parliament forbidding the killing of kittens in 2020. Vertical direct effect means that the United Kingdom would need to bring in an Act of Parliament that made it the law to kill all of the kittens (and the previous one would be repealed by the doctrine of 'implied repeal'). Now imagine that 2020 arrives, the United Kingdom has not

[78] UK House of Commons Library, International Affairs and Defence Section: 8. Standard Note: SN/IA/3689. *"Both the Council of Ministers and the Commission are empowered under the EC Treaty to make laws."*

done this and I am found in my back garden killing some kittens. Technically I am breaking the law, because the Act of Parliament forbidding the killing of kittens is still on the books, however by the doctrine of indirect effect, I am doing nothing wrong under European Law (which you will remember is supreme), because indirect effect comes into play when the member state has failed to introduce the directive, and thus places an obligation on the domestic courts to interpret the law in line with the European Union legislation. Indeed the United Kingdom could even be penalised in some way for not meeting the obligations set out in the directive.

When we examine a few examples of European Union law in action, we can see how it works and what the results can be. Naturally, these examples are not exhaustive given the enormous and impossible quantity that would have to be compiled here, but they highlight well some of the difficult areas of European Law and give us a clear indication of how our liberties are affected and how the European Union uses its position of supremacy in law for political gain.

In 2006, the European Union put into place the 'Shareholders' Rights Directive' which sought to encompass rights that could be considered fundamental to a shareholder. It replaced the previous 'First Company Law Directive' and contained such rights as; shareholders are to be given 21 days notice of meetings and companies are to facilitate electronic voting[79]; at meetings, no more than 5% of shareholders may table resolutions[80]; shareholders have a

---

[79] Shareholder Rights Directive 2007/36/EC ART 5

[80] Shareholder Rights Directive 2007/36/EC ART 6

right to ask questions[81]; to conduct proxy voting[82] and the result of votes should be publishable on the website of the respective company[83]. The Directive goes some way to recognising some of the fundamental rights summarised by Lord Wedderburn; for example the right to vote. It could be said then that the EU Directive does go some way towards clarifying the law on this issue, insofar as it tells us more clearly what rights cannot be taken away from a shareholder and any interference with these rights can bring a cause of action.

Some may claim that these rights and freedoms are helpful ones -indeed, in some respects they are! Other may point out how wonderful it is that the European Union is adopting and recognizing British company law principles, hence it is proof of their undying love for us, recognition of our ingenuity, and our own powerful influence. Of course, given the track record of the European Union, on a balance of probabilities this is probably utter nonsense.

Actually, it is worth noting that this is merely another example of the European Union enacting something that was already largely in place in the United Kingdom and perhaps other nations, as a means of not only transferring the administration and authority of these provisions, but also as a means of giving the appearance that such rights emanate from the European Union rather than domestic origins. Just like with the Human Rights Act, which as has been pointed out appear to simply codify liberties long established in the United Kingdom so as to appear to be the benevolent originator of them, so too the Shareholders

---

[81] Shareholder Rights Directive 2007/36/EC ART 9
[82] Shareholder Rights Directive 2007/36/EC ART 10
[83] Shareholder Rights Directive 2007/36/EC ART 14

Rights Directive appears to follow the same route. The result is that when a potential Brexit is put on the table, people will turn away in fear of losing their rights. Shareholders and investors in particular are important to any country, so the European Union of course seeks to give them the oppression that it is the Directive that protects them. Consequently, their ignorance of the fact English law protected them long before, just as it did with liberties, causes them to sway towards allegiance to the European Union. It is by any objective criteria, a perfectly constructed bit of hoodwinking. This Directive purports to grant some rights to shareholders, whilst really granting them nothing at all, so as to win over those institutions that are most likely to consist of shareholders, or have the most shareholders -namely, big corporations and big businesses.

Nevertheless, what of those who are involved in small businesses? It is well known that the European Union question creates a divide amongst business leaders, and a Poll in November 2015 carried out by YouGov, found that small and medium sized business leaders are more Eurosceptic than their large business counterparts[84]. This could partly be down to the sector of industry that the business is involved with, and how much expense, obstruction and inconvenience the overbearing red tape and immeasurable quantity of regulations causes to them. There are of course far too many rules, regulations, directives and laws that concern businesses; tens of thousands in fact —which is too many to list here. Nevertheless, to give an example of some of the infinitesimal elements of businesses that the European

---

[84] YouGov Poll. Business Sample 16th – 20th November 2015: PDF Format - https://d25d2506sfb94s.cloudfront.net/cumulus_uploads/document/npg64akeny/Results_for_Internal_21_1_16_Website.pdf

Union attempts to reign over, one can focus on just one or two examples.

Picture yourself as a small businessman working on a market stall or in a small shop. You most likely earn a modest living and spend your days selling your sought after wares to different types of people bustling around the busy high streets and marketplaces of the United Kingdom. You pay your tax, you pay your various taxes and you ensure your customers are happy; all in all, you mind your own business. In such a scenario it would be fair to say that the government should probably mind theirs too, as should the European Union. Indeed, historically in the United Kingdom, one of the great advantages that we have enjoyed by virtue of the prescribed rights and liberties that our negative liberty approach creates or grants, is that it encourages an entrepreneurial atmosphere. It is precisely this entrepreneurial atmosphere that allowed the United Kingdom to flourish over centuries, including during the industrial revolution, and made us one of the great powers of the world.

Adam Smith referred to us as *"a nation of shopkeepers[85]"* and it is the reason why even today we have rather a different approach to business and trade to our continental neighbours. This is why so many people, organisations and businesses want to come to the United Kingdom, have their financial headquarters here, or conduct their business through our superiorly trained expert agents. Entrepreneurship is another one of those concepts that is very much a British thing, and in turn, it stems from

---

[85] Smith, Adam; *The Wealth of Nations*, Glasgow edition, 1976), Book IV, section vii. c.

another British creation, that is individual liberty from a prescriptive or negative liberty viewpoint, which logically concludes in the right of an individual to conduct their own private business, to earn money, to live by earning a living. It is a wonderful and honourable trait of the British that we have long pioneered these approaches, which go much further than putting money in the pocket of ordinary men, but in fact keep the entire economy pumping and grant millions of people jobs, and with that, self-esteem and purpose.

Naturally though, the European Union sees things rather differently. Without any real recognition of prescribed rights, instead as we have discussed, preferring to take a positive liberty approach and uphold the idea of proscribed rights, the European Union cannot help but interfere even in the business of the small man on the market. They do not have any real regard for the individual rights and liberties of human beings, let alone when those rights stand in the way of even what is seemingly the minutest detail of European Union legislation. It matters little whether you are a mere market seller or shopkeeper, than your business has been established for generations, or that you pay your taxes, keep your customers happy and simply mind your own business. If you do not use your freedom of enterprise, or right to establish a business and earn a living, in the way that the European Union wishes for you to use it; if you do not exercise your liberties exactly as the European Union wants you to; then you are not only anathema to them, but you could well find that you have ceased to be a humble market seller minding his or her own business, and suddenly become a criminal! Perhaps this sounds extreme and thus unbelievable –indeed it is.

Nevertheless, it is real, and the case of *Thoburn v Sunderland City Council* proves exactly that.

The Weights and Measures Act 1985 is one of a vast number of Acts of Parliament that determined what measurements were recognized in law in the United Kingdom[86]. In reality, Acts of Parliament governing measurements go back centuries, but in the *Thoburn* case it is this Act, which was good law at the time, that matters. The fundamentals of this Act was that it gave a certain freedom of choice to businesses as to what measurements they used by recognizing in law, both pounds and kilos, as equal and acceptable. Naturally an example of the British' practical and pragmatic approach, which as a consequence of recognizing both, enabled small business to avoid the huge costs of changing or reconfiguring weighing equipment and undergoing other costs and restructures, whilst giving those new business or larger organisations the option of changing or using both. It was a flexible approach that struck a useful balance between giving clarity on legal measurements, which was good for the consumer, whilst giving fluidity and choice for the business, which aided small businesses and promoted a more plural level of co-operation. Nonetheless, as I mentioned before, and as I am sure is becoming increasingly apparent to you by now, the pragmatism of a law is not the European Union's concern; their only concern is their agenda of further harmonization of law for a purpose much more significant than mere citizens or individuals such as you or I; for a European super state with overreaching power, using the best method for the job, the law and legal system.

In 1979, Directive 80/181 was introduced as to substitute

---

[86] Weights and Measures Act 1985 - http://www.legislation.gov.uk/ukpga/1985/72

for Directive 71/354[87]. The main purposes of the new Directive 80/181 was four fold; firstly it required that many of the units of measurement that were permitted under the previous Directive were allowed to stay in use until 1985, by which time they would then have to be removed. Another aim was that, as was particularly relevant to the United Kingdom, pound, ounces, gallons, pints, inches, yard and foot, would be permitted until the very end of 1989 by which time they would be phased out. Additionally, the other two points permitted the use of imperial measurements on signs, land and buildings; and allowed the use of supplementary units.

As has been made clear in my previous explanation on Directives, the nature of this method of introducing law to member states works by setting a desired aim and then giving member states a date by which that aim should be achieved, through law. In the case of the United Kingdom, this of course meant passing an Act of Parliament; this was done, in the form of the Weights and Measures Act 1985 (Metrication) (Amendment) Order 1994, along with the Units of Measurement Regulations 1994. Resultantly then, United Kingdom law was knocked firmly into line with the requirements set out in Directive 80/181. Of course this was done with absolutely no regard for any concept or potential argument for the right or liberty of an individual to use their own measurement in business, nor the operational costs to small businesses or difficulty culturally in adjusting to these new measurements. That isn't

---

[87] *Council Directive 80/181/EEC of 20 December 1979 on the approximation of the laws of the Member States relating to units of measurement and on the repeal of Directive 71/354/EEC, OJ L 39, 15.2.1980, p. 40–50*

important of course, because as has become clearer and clearer in our investigation, the European Union is fundamentally anti-libertarian.

Enter Steve Thoburn, a humble, average greengrocer from Sunderland. In July of 2000, on an ordinary business day, Mr. Thoburn was busy running his shop in order to earn his bread and butter. Mr. Thoburn was paying his taxes, serving his customers and providing a business to his local community like he would do on any other day. A customer entered Mr. Thoburn's shop and purchased some bananas from Mr. Thoburn and quickly left the shop. Yet little time had passed since the customer had left the shop, before Mr. Thoburn received a visit from two officers representing Trading Standards. It transpired, that Mr. Thoburn, upon selling those bananas, had gone from being that humble greengrocer we met a short time ago, to being a hardened criminal. His crime? Using pounds to weigh the bananas. As a result of Mr. Thoburn's heinous criminal activity, the two officers attempted to seize his weighing equipment which was prohibited, and after some understandable protesting from Mr. Thoburn, managed to do so, but not without enlisting the help of two police officers who threatened him with arrest if he did not allow the equipment to be taken. It emerged that the initial customer was no customer at all, but rather, an undercover officer working for Sunderland Council —just in case you wondered what kind of things your tax money goes on. The council in question later made the decision to prosecute Mr. Thoburn for his 'disgraceful' behaviour. Perhaps there were a shortage of rapists, murderers and terrorists in 2000 —you never know!

It is worth pausing for a moment, to reflect on exactly what had happened here. We are looking at an incident where two police officers and two trading standards officer, along with an undercover officer, entered the private business premises of a humble greengrocer trying to earn a probably modest wage, seized his equipment and later arrested and prosecuted him, all because he was using the pounds weight unit as opposed to the kilos. If you do not see the incredible, fascist-scale disproportionality of this, then you have a serious problem. A fundamental principle behind the very idea of negative civil liberties, freedoms and rights, going back centuries to the Charter of Liberties and Magna Carta that we mentioned before, is that rather than the government proscribing what you may do, they instead tell you what you cannot do, and this would usually be based on the philosophy that you may do as you please provided it does not cause physical or property damage, or a breach of the liberties of another. A victimless crime should never be considered a crime in the first place; it should be considered a freedom, a liberty, and a right, because by virtue of being victimless, it is in essence doing no harm or damage to any other. Yet the authorities dragged Mr. Thoburn through the criminal courts, granting him the wonderful gift of a criminal record for the remainder of his life. They took a good, hardworking, harmless man who was literally minding his own business, and purposely turned him into a criminal.

Yet who was the victim? Who was this law designed to protect? What was the purpose of removing Mr. Thoburn's liberties in the way one would expect the liberties of a murderer or terrorist to be removed (and sadly in a way they often aren't)? Where was the Human Right's Act to protect him? The great swathes of question marks seem to wash over this case like an enormous sea of confusion and despair whenever one ponders the underlying principles and motives behind the states actions. In truth however, if we are honest with ourselves and dismiss our optimistic naivety, deep down we know that the real reason why these actions were taken and why this law was introduced in the first place, was because the European Union had an agenda of 'ever closer union', and they were so obsessed with it that it boiled right down to the extremities, minutiae and details of even the private business of innocent small business owners. It was not a question of justice, fairness, liberty or proportionality; this was all about making an example of one man who dared to use a different set of weights to the one that the European Union had told him he could use.

The Labour party proponents of the working class however, were nowhere to be seen in defending this working man, in fact they were not only disinterested in shielding this innocent worker from the blows of the European Union's hammer of dogma that were crashing down on his life, liberty and business, but they were completely complicit in it. After all, it was Labour who introduced this measure and then proceeded to enforce it; it was a Labour Party Government and a Labour Party Council. If it wasn't clear already then, that the allegiances of the 'Party of the Working Class' lies with those who may offer them a higher job and more authority –the EU, then it at least begins the show now. Mr. Thoburn had to tell his staff not to come into work, hand over his property, and face the full force of the criminal justice system as if he had been dealing drugs. Mr. Thoburn's life was being ruined purely as a result of those in positions of power wanting to stamp down their agenda and make an example for everyone else.

Do not think for a moment though, that the saga ends here. In fact, it gets even more insane and terrifying. There was a slight problem, legally, with the logic of Mr. Thoburn's charges, which lay in the judgment of the court that was itself immensely controversial, and not in the positive way, that it provoked outrage across the nation. Not that outrage was particularly of any importance to the European Union; public outrage is a problem for domestic governments to deal with as far as the European Union is concerned, they are the 'fall guys' for the European Union and they gladly take up the position, probably in the hope of doing an impressive job and securing a high ranking, well paid, European Union bureaucrat position. Even with the recent tampon tax scandal there were protests against the Tory Government taxing feminine hygiene products, seemingly in complete ignorance of the fact that this tax is grounded in European Union law and therefore it is the European Union taxing these products outside of domestic control. Interesting to note then, that neither the European Union nor the Government really made any huge issue out of this fact, but the Prime Minister did manage to abolish it, after begging to Brussels of course. What a wonderful democracy -what an influential country we are!

Part of the great significance constitutionally, and in turn with regards to liberty, of *Thoburn v Sunderland City Council* is that the appellants (people making the appeal) made use of perfectly valid constitutional conventions in order to attempt to protect themselves and to limit the government. The appellants claimed that the weights and measures regulations that were being used to convict them were invalid. Their reasoning made use of the constitutional and legal convention of the 'doctrine of implied repeal'. Whilst common law is overruled by statute in the form of acts of Parliament, thus any contradictions in law are settled; the doctrine of implied repeal concerns situations where two acts of Parliament are in conflict. In these circumstances, where two acts conflict or contradict, the doctrine of implied repeal dictates that the earlier act is impliedly repealed by virtue of the introduction of the new act, thus the new acts abrogates the earlier act, or at least the conflicting section of it.

What relevance did this have to the *Thoburn* case? Well, the weights and measures regulations of the European Union, were, as noted above, introduced via a directive. As we know, directives do not have direct effect; instead they place an obligation on the state to achieve a particular result by a particular time, but leave the ways and means up to the discretion of the member state. As we know, the authority that Parliament has for introducing European Union legislation into domestic law, comes from the European Communities Act 1972. Section 2(2) of this act is the section that permits Ministers to adopt secondary legislation (that is to say legislation from the European Union) into United Kingdom's law[88]. Applying that to this case, the court that had ruled against Mr. Thoburn by giving legal effective to the directive because of the fact that this act gives authority to European Union law, and European Union law is, as we have established, supreme. Nevertheless, the Weights and Measures Act directly conflicted with the European Union law that the European

---

[88] *European Communities Act 1972*, S. 2(2) -
http://www.legislation.gov.uk/ukpga/1972/68/section/2

Communities Act 2(2) was giving effect to as secondary legislation, since it permitted both kilos and pounds to be used. Consequently, Thoburn argued that Parliament's introduction of the Weights and Measures Act in 1994, and its subsequent amendments, were in direct conflict with the very act being used to implement the European Union's Directive (European Communities Act), therefore by virtue of the doctrine of implied repeal, section 2(2) of the European Communities Act had been impliedly repealed as far as the topic of the directive (weights and measures), and was therefore invalid; rendering the directive unenforceable[89].

If we are completely honest, this is a very good argument. Consider it, if the European Communities Act is passed in 1972 and contains a provision that allows ministers to give effect to secondary legislation, and they then pass an act in conflict with that legislation, then it stands to reason that there is conflict with the act of parliament giving effect to the secondary legislation. Consequently, if the doctrine of implied repeal suggests that earlier statutes replaces the sections of older statutes that it conflicts with, then that act of parliament giving effect to the secondary legislation with which the newer act conflicts, is surely impliedly repealed just like any other act?

This was just one of a few arguments that Thoburn used, and it was a very good one indeed. However, this argument and all of the other arguments that were used failed to win him the appeal. Unfortunately, the European Law extended so far that it could intervene directly in some of the age-old

---

[89] *Thoburn v Sunderland City Council* [2002] 3 WLR 247, [2002] EWHC 195 (Admin), [2003] QB 151

and almost flawless constitutional conventions of our own nation. The judge in the case argued that there were in fact a number of constitutional statutes, which includes the European Communities Act 1972. These statutes could not be impliedly repealed because of their importance, and so as a result, the only way to repeal these statutes would be through express repeal. The judge ruled that the *Factortame* case, where Parliament had passed the Merchant Shipping Act 1988 which had impliedly repealed section 2(2) of the European Communities Act[90], had already dealt with this problem. In this case, the House of Lords had already held that implied repeal did not work here. This may have been one of the reasons that after the Court of Appeal, the House of Lords (now the Supreme Court) rejected an application from Thoburn for further appeal. It seems to me, to be rather stretching logic to assume, and I believe it quite evident that it is an assumption, that Parliament did not intend to repeal the Act with respect to weights and measures[91].

In my view, if the intention is quite evident and clear, then surely an express repeal is somewhat unnecessary. Why would our own Parliament pass a law that makes an explicit provision for both pounds and kilos to be given equality in law, if they also had no intention of repealing the requirements of section 2(2) that meant implement law that was explicitly to the contrary? What would be the point? It is akin to some individual smashing some windows through on a closed shop and going inside, then denying that there

---

[90]R *(Factortame Ltd) v Secretary of State for Transport*, [2000] EWHC 179

[91] *Thoburn v Sunderland City Council* [2002] 3 WLR 247, [2002] EWHC 195 (Admin), [2003] QB 151 (Judgment)

is any reasonable basis on which to suggest he intended to rob it, or even break into it. The fact is that his actions, and the fact that they are so clear and explicit, demonstrate what he intends to do. The same principle surely applies here; Parliament's actions in implementing a law that goes so far as to have wording to the contrary of another, surely intend for that law to be implemented.

Once again, we can see the effect of granting European Union law, as created mostly by the unelected and unaccountable, being supreme over a far more experienced and even-handed system. European Union Law had continued in its tradition of trampling on the rights of the small man in its obsessive micromanagement of individual liberties and lives; and our own domestic courts had been shackled, unable to resist or to uphold the liberties of the United Kingdom and her people.

Mr. Thoburn's life was ruined. Mr. Thoburn became known as the original *Metric Martyr* but he was not by any means the only person prosecuted as a result of this Directive, in fact, there were several others. Julian Harman, a fruit seller from Cornwall, was convicted for the scandalous act of setting his Apples' price at 45 pence to the pound; John Dove, a fishmonger who was also from Cornwall, dared to sell mackerel at £1.54 per pound, the horror! Additionally, Peter Collins from Sutton, whilst never prosecuted, challenged his Council's threats to revoke his street trading licence as a result of using illegal weighing equipment, in court; he lost. Whilst London based Colin Hunt received a 12 month conditional discharge for failing to display the per kilo price of sweet potatoes. All of these people became criminals, simply by virtue of the fact that the European Union didn't like the weights they were using!

CHAPTER 10
WORKERS RIGHTS? WHAT RIGHTS?

One of the most common pieces of fear mongering –and it is indeed fear mongering- is that Brexit will result in a mass elimination of worker's rights. Apparently, some have the idea that the European Union is the reason why we have such rights as maternity pay, annual leave, sick pay and such like. The European Union is somehow the great safeguard of worker's wellbeing and cares so deeply about us all, except of course if you're a metric martyr that it endeavours always to protect us from the tyranny of our own oppressive Parliament. 'Nonsense' is the only word that can be used to respond to such claims.

Unfortunately, the Unions are convinced of, or at least act to peddle these myths. The assistant General Secretary of the Irish Congress of Trade Unions (ICTU) claimed that;

> *'It is worth noting, however, that our membership of the EU acts to underpin workers' rights across the UK, and if the Tory right succeed in dragging Northern Ireland away from the EU then it would be easier for them to drag down the legal*

entitlements won by workers all across the UK [92]."

The idea that somehow the European Union underpins workers' rights is really quite baseless. He is not alone however, Frances O'Grady of the Trade Union Congress also claims that; *"working people have a huge stake in the referendum because workers' rights are on the line [93]".* In actual fact, there is far less evidence to suggest this is true than the contrary point which is that the United Kingdom, and yes, including the Tories, have long exceeded the requirements laid out in European Union Law; sometimes they have even predated them.

Workers' rights are actually yet another example of the expansion of liberty in the United Kingdom. Indeed, it was the United Kingdom that pioneered worker's and labour rights, once again long before other nations followed suit. Just as was highlight previously, regarding the Human Rights Act, where the Europhiles frequently try to act in a way that gives us the impression that our liberties and rights emanate from the European Union when in reality our continental cousins fail to even remotely understand any real concept of liberty; the same is true in this case.

The Equal Pay Act was introduced in the United Kingdom in 1970[94], which was several years before we joined the common market. There are those who claim that there is

---

[92] Belfast Telegraph; *Brexit would threaten workers' rights in Northern Ireland, says union leader,* [29th April 2016], Retrieved 30th April 2016 -
http://www.belfasttelegraph.co.uk/news/northern-ireland/brexit-would-threaten-workers-rights-in-northern-ireland-says-union-leader-34670949.html
[93] The Guardian; *Workers' rights are on the line in EU referendum, warns TUC,* [25TH February 2016], Retrieved 3rd March 2016 -
http://www.theguardian.com/politics/2016/feb/25/workers-rights-are-on-the-line-in-eu-referendum-warns-tuc
[94] *Equal Pay Act 1970* (Now mostly superceded by the Equality Act 2010, Part 5, C.3) -
http://www.legislation.gov.uk/ukpga/1970/41

still a great scale of pay inequality amongst several professions in particular, which is a different debate, but the fact remains that it was the United Kingdom that pioneered the idea in this country, not the European Union. Indeed, suppose those who claim the Equal Pay Act has had little effect were correct, where are the European Union laws that are forcing the United Kingdom government to act? Whichever way one considers the situation, the European Union does not come out clean. On the one hand, the Equal Pay Act shows that the European Union is not responsible for the salary rights of employees, but that they are homegrown. On the other hand, any presence of unequal pay that exists in the United Kingdom, demonstrates that the European Union itself is ineffective and uninterested in upholding that fundamental right.

There is also a question of logic that lies in this question. Do we really think that the United Kingdom's government, upon Brexit, are going to suddenly call for the abolition of sick leave? Are we really so inept as a country that we cannot legislate or keep legislation, in accordance with the desires we have for worker's rights? Where did this idea come from, that the nation who pioneered liberty, and indeed expanded it to worker's rights as early as the 18th century, are suddenly more prone to oppressing their workforce than the European Union? Actually, things like the requirements of companies to publish their gender pay gaps, the national living wage, apprentice levies or payroll taxes all come from the United Kingdom's own government as opposed to the European Union. So if you support these things, it should rather be the Conservative government you might wish to thank. Whether you support them or not though, it is important to note that whilst the

European Union doesn't prevent them, it certainly hasn't implemented them. In fact, the United Kingdom continually exceeds the minimum requirements laid down by the European Union, it does so under no compulsion. If the United Kingdom's government wished, it could grant you only 20 days' holiday as the European Union requires, but instead it gives you a minimum of 28 days.

In fact, the United Kingdom has a long track record of pioneering children's, worker's and labour rights, independently of the European Union and at a time when many would expect us to have been far less socially minded. Free school meals were permitted in the United Kingdom from 1906 onwards[95]; 1908 saw the introduction of the *Children's Charter*, which in true British style was the first of its kind and protected children from neglect and cruelty as well as exploitation, it even created separate prisons known as *borstals* and outlawed selling cigarettes to children[96]. These two provisions had the effect of assisting working families who had children to feed and care for, and who were most affected by poverty. We also brought in the Trades Disputes Act in 1906, which supported the right to strike, along with the Worker's Compensation Act, which entitled people to compensation for workplace injuries[97]. On top of this, we introduced pensions as early as 1908 as well as regulating minor's working days to an eight-hour shift; and we also saw *labour exchanges* in 1909 to assist people in finding jobs or work. 1910 granted half a day a week off for shop workers, which was quite a large amount

---

[95] Education (Provision of Meals) Act 1906 -
http://www.legislation.gov.uk/ukpga/1906/57/enacted
[96] Children Act 1908 -
http://www.legislation.gov.uk/ukpga/Edw7/8/67/contents/enacted
[97] Trade Disputes And Trade Unions Act 1946 -
http://www.legislation.gov.uk/ukpga/Geo6/9-10/52/contents

for the time. The United Kingdom even went as far as to introduce measures in 1911 to ensure that working men could stand for election.

Also in 1911 we saw the introduction of the National Insurance Act, which entitled people to universal and free healthcare as well as sick leave and unemployment benefit. It seems to me a rather strange assertion to make then, that the European Union would be held up as the bastion of worker's rights in the United Kingdom, when almost all of the rights that workers, children and the elderly enjoy even to this very day, are as a result of the United Kingdom's own pioneering outlook and our own Parliament, not the European Union. It seems that the same misleading rhetoric is used for worker's rights, as for individual or civil liberties, and once again it is a lie. I would argue that despite words written in various Directives to the contrary, in reality the European Union is the enabler of oppression of workers, through some rather sneaky means.

One of the founding principles of the European Union, is the Free Movement of People[98]. This means that along with goods and services, people may move freely between member states to live, study or work, or in some cases - although I would concede a minority, not work, without the usual immigration or visa restrictions placed on them. The implications of this are legally, constitutionally and in relation to workers' rights, astounding. What is even more astounding is the amount of people who supposedly believe in worker's rights, who instead choose to close their eyes and cover their ears to the huge issues, preferring to

---

[98] *Article 3(2) of the Treaty on European Union (TEU); Article 21 of the Treaty on the Functioning of the European Union (TFEU); Titles IV and V TFEU.*

repeat the 'Stronger In' mantra until they've convinced themselves accordingly. Naturally this helps nobody, but it was never about that, the European Union dream is not interested in job losses or death tolls, not when they cannot profit politically from it.

How does the free movement of people affect your individual liberties, or worker's rights? Well the response is quite straightforward. The country has a finite amount of resources, with a finite amount of jobs, yet there is at least comparatively the equivalent of an infinite number of people who can come here. As many as half of the approximate 330,000 immigrants who came here in the last year, are European Union citizens[99].

One way that mass immigration affects worker's rights is with wages. The Bank of England published a report that pointed out the huge quantity of arrivals from the European Union was driving wages down, it stated; *"...as immigration rises by 10%, wages fall by 0.3%[100]."* The reason this happens, is because of course those people from European Union member states with a minimum wage that is only a minute fraction of ours are more likely to take advantage of the freedom of movement that membership of the European Union bestows upon them. In turn, jobs that used to pay a higher wage than the United Kingdom's minimum will be given to these new arrivals at minimum wage, which in turn causes a type of domino effect that can be felt across the board. Human labour, like any other

[99] Office For National Statistics; *Migration Statistics Quarterly Report:* February 2016-
http://www.ons.gov.uk/peoplepopulationandcommunity/populationandmigration/int
ernationalmigration/bulletins/migrationstatisticsquarterlyreport/february2016
[100] Nickell Stephen; and Saleheen Jumana; *The Impact of Immigration on Occupational Wages – Evidence from Britain*, December 2015, Staff Working Paper No. 574 (PDF Format: http://www.bankofengland.co.uk/research/Documents/workingpapers/2015/swp574.pdf)

commodity in a market-based economy, is determined primarily (but not exclusively) by its scarcity and complexity. Consequently, a job that used to pay £10 per hour, might now be offered at £7.20 an hour. This attracts more people, and thus we see a saturation of the jobs market where there are many more jobseekers than jobs. As a result, more jobs are offered at a lower wage and United Kingdom workers, which consists of those already here or those born here, must compete. Inevitably, wages fall, and wage compression takes effect; this affects all workers, in every field.

The Government's plans for a national living wage will not work to alleviate this problem; in fact, it will make it worse. Raising the minimum wage will simply attract more immigrants from poorer European countries and further compress wages across the board. In the process, it may also make it impossible for smaller companies to employ enough staff, and so they too will be negatively affected. Still –it is such a small price to play for the European Union dream, right? The truth is that the only way we can truly uphold worker's rights is by limiting the amount of labour that is saturating the market and causing wage compression. We cannot do this when we do not even have proper sovereignty over our own borders; without limiting immigration and being able to select based on our own requirements and skills shortages, wages will continue to fall and the standard of living with it.

Furthermore, what about the amount of money that is paid out of your pocket to the European Union for the privilege of having them rule your life? Taxation most definitely concerns the individual, and indeed one could argue that unless you have economic freedom or autonomy, you do not have freedom at all. It is perfectly well and good for a government to grant you rights and tell you that you are free, but it is meaningless when they remove your resources to exercise that freedom through unjustifiable tax. The European Union is paid for out of our taxes. The way in which our contribution of £11,000,000,000 per year is calculated is based on a tax that you pay every single day, often several times a day; Value Added Tax (VAT).

European Union contributions are calculated based on the VAT intake of a government by virtue of the VAT Directive[101]. This places an extra 20% onto the cost of most of your weekly shopping so that we can be a net contributor to the European Union. Being a net contributor means that we pay in more than we get out, even without any rebates, and so you are essentially paying more for your groceries and receiving little to nothing in return. Even the so-called 'tampon tax' which was not exempt from VAT, was blamed on the government when in reality it comes from the European Union. Still, thankfully our Prime Minister was able to beg for a change to this tax, and graciously given it, how generous. Remember, this contribution is separate from the contribution your taxes make to a failing Eurozone that has unemployment at several times the percentage that we do, with Greece and Spain both with unemployment rates at over 20% as of January 2016[102].

The cost of living rising, and the income of the average

---

[101] *Council Directive 2006/112/EC of 28 November 2006 on the common system of value added tax* OJ L 347, 11.12.2006, p. 1–118

[102] *Eurostat* stastics, *Unemployment Statistics up to March 2016*, Retrieved 30th April 2016 (correct at time of retrieval) - http://ec.europa.eu/eurostat/statistics-explained/index.php/Unemployment_statistics

household falling, represents just two issues that really do affect workers' rights, which can be attributed to European Union membership. Without the legal right to take control of these things, we will not be able to fix the problem. If we do take control of our own laws governing the border, we know from history that we can trust those laws to protect worker's rights because they have done so for over a century. Don't just take it from me though! Even Stuart Rose, the head of the Remain campaign has admitted that in the event of Brexit, wages will rise, although he doesn't think that is necessarily a positive thing[103].

This is hardly surprising given the remain camp are a group of people who watch the United Kingdom's steel industry collapse, with the United Government unable to help due to European Rules. Rules that prevent nationalization or bailouts; and continue to support European Union membership nonetheless. Margaret Vestager, the EU Commissioner responsible for competition policy in the European Union commented directly on the steel crisis that endangers so many British jobs;

"EU countries and the Commission have put in place strict safeguards against state aid to rescue and restructure steel companies in difficulty [104]."

Tell me more about how the European Union's levies and laws are helping United Kingdom worker's rights?

[103] The Daily Telegraph; *Wages for British workers will rise in the event of a Brexit, head of 'in' campaign Lord Rose says*, [3rd March 2016], Retrieved 12th April 2016 - http://www.telegraph.co.uk/news/newstopics/eureferendum/12181385/Wages-for-British-workers-will-rise-in-the-event-of-a-Brexit-head-of-in-campaign-says.html
[104] BBC NEWS; *UK steel industry and the EU debate*, [30th March 2016], Retrieved 2nd April 2016 - http://www.bbc.co.uk/news/uk-politics-35927542

Dominic Bardill

CHAPTER 11
ANOTHER 'TRANSATLANTIC TRADE'

One of the most controversial topics in the European Union debate at present, is the subject of TTIP. TTIP stands for the Transatlantic Trade and Investment Partnership . It is a deal that the European Union are currently negotiating with the United States of America as you read this. At first thought, it seems perfectly legitimate and even positive that we would be pursuing free trade agreements with such a huge and influential country as the United States. Indeed, as someone who personally supports free trade and free markets, I should be relatively supportive of TTIP —but I'm not. In fact, TTIP in my opinion is an absolutely atrocious and disgraceful plan, which every single person across the European continent and in particular the United Kingdom, should be terrified about. My reasoning behind it is as follows.

TTIP is entirely secret. When I say secret, I mean literally secret right down to the very details and documents that will form the contract or treaty arrangements. Molly Scott Cato is the MEP for South West England; for the officially pro-European Union Green Party no less! She described a scene in her article in the Guardian, which should indicate to you just how secret TTIP really is, and I would hope by now that you can spot for yourself the horrific implications that lie in its secrecy.

> *"I have now been granted privileged access to the European parliament restricted reading room to explore documents relating to the Transatlantic Trade and Investment Partnership (TTIP) deal. But before I had the right to see such "top secret" documents, which are restricted from the gaze of most EU citizens, I was required to sign a document of some 14 pages, reminding me that "EU institutions are a valuable target" and of the dangers of espionage. Crucially, I had to agree not to share any of the contents with those I represent [105]."*

Clear proof of the secrecy of TTIP is to be found mostly in the final sentence; *"Crucially, I had to agree not to share any of the contents with those I represent [106]."* So to clarify, the only people who are allowed access to the documents of this trade proposal are businesspeople, and MEPs. MEPs are of course, banned from sharing any of the information on which their eyes settle with any of the people who elected them to the European Parliament. This alone should indicate that the contents have a nature that most members of the European electorate would never approve, indeed the very fact that the European Union is removing the capacity of an MEP to represent their constituents, is breath-taking –is this not defeating the very purpose of having MEPs? Instead, the EU has compiled its own two page summaries of TTIP, which are available on the

---

[105] Cato, Molly Scott (In the Guardian), *'I've seen the secrets of TTIP, and it is built for corporations not citizens'*, [4th February 2015], Retrieved 2nd April 2016. - http://www.theguardian.com/commentisfree/2015/feb/04/secrets-ttip-corporations-not-citizens-transatlantic-trade-deal
[106] ^ibid

European Union website, and these summaries carefully select bits of information that the public are allowed to know. We can assume that this twisted, spun or reworded so as to fool the average person.

In light of the fact that TTIP is secret, there is little information available on which to base criticisms or scrutiny; I would suggest the very top secret nature of it should set enough alarm bells off for any reasonably sane person though. Nevertheless, *Greenpeace* recently leaked a series of documents that exposed TTIP[107]. I have had the privilege of looking at these restricted documents, which you can also see for yourself, and they do not paint a positive picture. Using these leaked documents, and taking information from similar deals the USA has with other countries, we can gain an indication as to what TTIP represents. The results are really quite shocking.

TTIP contains plans to introduce the European Union's new *Investment Court System'* (otherwise known as an Investor-State Dispute Settlement or ISDS) . These special courts would be designed to settle disputes between investors and states, overriding our own courts and ignoring the fact that English law, in all its superiority, has long been a favourite for contractual, trade and financial law the world over. These new courts system would grant rights to corporations to bring action in court against individual member states, where those member states' laws negatively affect investment or reduce profits for that corporation[108].

---

[107] Greenpeace, RESTRICTED: National Treatment for Market Access and Goods, (*Leaked TTIP Documents)*, Retrieved 2nd May 2016 - https://www.ttip-leaks.org/
[108] ^Ibid

To give an example of how serious this could be , imagine if the United Kingdom government outlawed a certain unhealthy or potentially dangerous food ingredient that a fast food company like McDonalds were using. Under these new arrangements, if this theoretical legislation meant that McDonalds received less investment, or lost profit as a result of having to buy new stock or change their recipe, then they could sue the United Kingdom government for ridiculously large sums of money. I am sure you will agree, the potential for exploitation ISDS has is unacceptable.

Regard for a moment, the actions of the French Supreme Court recently. In April 2015, the French Supreme Court (Conseil D'Etat) overruled a 2014 legislative order banning the cultivation of a genetically modified corn produced by the American company, *Monsanto*. The cultivation of this same corn had previously been authorised by the European Commission back in 1998. The Supreme Court based its judgment on the European Food Safety Authority's claim that there is not enough evidence that genetically modified corn implies more risk than conventional corn[109]. Now, my point is not to expand on whether or not the corn is in fact harmful to human health or the environment, but rather, to highlight an important and worrying aspect of this ruling. What the court's actions show, are the dangerous dynamics of European legislation in exercising the supremacy they have obtained, over domestic laws. The elected French government was denied the right to implement a law that went against what Brussels had dictated. Now, this is

---

[109] France.info, '*Le Conseil d'État annule l'arrêté interdisant le maïs transgénique MON810*', [15th April 2016], Retrieved 30th April 2016 -http://www.franceinfo.fr/fil-info/article/le-conseil-d-etat-annule-l-arrete-interdisant-le-mais-genetiquement-modifie-mon-810-communique-782595

indeed nothing new or surprising, and should not be a shock to you by now. However, in relation to TTIP, this is particularly worrisome; if it happened to France, it can happen to the United Kingdom and so it seriously endangers the liberties and autonomy that we have so passionately shaped for ourselves over the centuries.

Another example of the European Union using its lawmaking powers to pander to United States corporatism as a preference over -and to the detriment of- the individual, dates back to 2015. The European Commission authorised the importation and commercialisation of nineteen different kinds of genetically modified crops. There were eleven from the controversial *Monsanto*. In an illogical move only found in bureaucracies like the European Union, a reform was offered to member states that would enable them to 'protection' themselves against those genetically modified crops if they wished to. The reason this was so illogical, and frivolous, was because in a zone of free-trade, where decisions are ultimately made above the heads of member states, those protections would be practically ineffective[110].

Yet, the most ludicrous aspect of the story is that the United States openly voiced its dissatisfaction with regards to the European Union's 'fence-sitting'. They would have liked the European Union to impose the crops more forcibly[111]. Naturally, being interested only in corporatism

---

[110] Le Figaro, *'L'Union européenne autorise 19 OGM et met tout le monde en colère'*, [25th April 2015], Retrieved 30th April 2016 - http://www.lefigaro.fr/sciences/2015/04/24/01008-20150424ARTFIG00413-l-union-europeenne-autorise-19-ogm-et-met-tout-le-monde-en-colere.php

[111] ^iBid

and power, the European Union would place the United States' corporatist interests first. Whilst, to any fair-minded and self-respecting law-making institution, the interests of American corporations should not come into consideration when deciding on our own national fates, yet this is exactly what is happening in Brussels, which is the second worldwide capital for lobbying after Washington DC.

In the light of such examples, I can only invite you to entertain what would happen once TTIP comes into being. This would be the final blow to our democratic aspirations, and we as individuals would be left watching, as it crumble under the weight of corporate interests. Whether you are left wing, right wing or centrist, you can never justify a position where a Supreme Court is answerable to a European Union that shows allegiance to American corporations over the wellbeing of the individual member states and their peoples. I remind you of one of the founding provisions in the Maastricht Treaty which stresses that the European Union was;

> "...founded on the values of respect for human dignity, freedom, democracy, equality, the rule of law and respect for human rights, including the rights of persons belonging to minorities [112]."

Where is the respect for human dignity? Where is the freedom? Importantly and perhaps more pertinently, where is the rule of law and the democracy? If McDonalds can sue our democratically elected government, and if the French Supreme Court is already surrendering in advance (no surprise there!) to a top-secret corporatism document, then none of the claims regarding the values that the

---

[112] Article 2, *Treaty on the European Union,* OJ C 326, 26.10.2012, p. 13–390

European Union claim to have hold any credibility. Well, in case you had not realised by now, the European Union is not really concerned with your country's freedoms or liberties, let alone yours! In fact, of all of the secret negotiations regarding TTIP that the European Union organised, 92% of the time involved meetings between the business leaders and the European Commission[113]; MEPs, MPs, member states, trade union officials etc. were almost never invited to give their opinions of feedback. That should tell you everything you need to know.

In fact, to really stress the seriousness of this point to you, it is worth informing you that so far under similar systems, the corporations from the United States have sued the Canadian Government for billions of dollars. These cases have involved the Canadian Government banning certain medicines, introducing certain rules, and denying licences to various corporations. Perhaps it is important, if you are someone who values your liberties, to consider how this affects you personally for a moment.

Presume for a moment, that the NHS decided that they deemed a certain drug to be unsafe and so the government put a suspension on the issuing of that medicine to members of the public. If it were a Japanese company for example, then this would not be an issue, simply tough luck for the company. However, if the company was a United States enterprise then TTIP would entitle them to sue the British Government. The issues they could sue the government over include compensation for the damaging of their investments if they were affected, compensation for damage done to the company's reputation, breach of

---

[113] Corporate Europe Observatory; *Who lobbies most on TTIP?*, [June 8th 2014], International Trade, Retrieved February 28th 2015 - http://corporateeurope.org/international-trade/2014/07/who-lobbies-most-ttip

contract and even loss of profit[114].

Consider for a moment two ways that this stitch up could effect you personally: It would inevitably lead to the complete privatisation of the NHS and other public services into American hands which would affect each and every person who uses it, which I presume includes yourself. Note that it would not even be privatisation under British oversight, but American oversight. Secondly, it would open the NHS and other public services up to huge lawsuits that could push them to the verge of bankruptcy. When the NHS is already facing a stream of immense crises, opening it up to the risk of lawsuits from the United States is quite frankly a preposterous proposal, but TTIP supports that proposal nonetheless.

Aside from the fact that the effective sale of the NHS would affect you as an individual member of British society, there is another important and simple point of which you need to take notice. A lawsuit against the United Kingdom's government is a lawsuit against the United Kingdom's taxpayers, considering the United Kingdom has taxes in just about every area including consumption taxes, this means a lawsuit against each and every one of us. In short, TTIP will allow the United States to seize control of our public services and sue you by proxy if our Government does not comply; and with whose help? Well, the European Union's of course!

The potential risks with TTIP do not end there unfortunately. Another known aspect of this agreement is that it will effectively bring corporations into the legislature.

---

[114] Greenpeace, RESTRICTED: National Treatment for Market Access and Goods, (*Leaked TTIP Documents*), Retrieved 2nd May 2016 - https://www.ttip-leaks.org/

Of course this won't be done officially, instead it will be by proxy that huge corporations will have the ability to assist in the drafting of new legislation. The term that is used in TTIP-style agreements for giving companies such power, is 'regulatory cooperation' . It involves huge businesses being permitted to send representatives to meet with other representatives to help in drafting laws that have not even reached the Parliamentary stage yet[115].

Enough members of the public are quite sick of lobbying in Westminster already, few realise that the European Union is one of the worst institutions for lobbying, but TTIP will mean that there won't be much need for it, since they are going to invite organisations like Apple to help write the laws that regulate them! If there was ever a way to undermine democracy, and the sovereignty of Parliaments or nations, then this is one! How does it affect you as an individual? It allows your elected representatives to be undermined and essentially influenced by big business. These businesses will have more of a whip hand over your own Parliament that you do! Ask yourself if this is ever acceptable; ask yourself if a European Union that supports and is even complicit in such behavior, is a European Union you wish to be a part of.

We have already seen the utter contempt that the European Union holds for small and medium sized business owners. We have witnessed already in the story of Mr. Thoburn that the European Union is more than willing to trample individual members of our society over the smallest of matters. Imagine how they will behave when TTIP comes into play. We will not only see a drop in food standards as the American system for food regulation and risk

---

[115] ^Ibid

assessment is introduced; something that the United States is apparently pushing for; but we will also see further trampling over the liberties of those smaller businesses that need our support. The nature of the TTIP deal is such that it will benefit enormous corporations at the expense of all other groups like never before.

This is not a free market, and it is not capitalism, it is corporatism and monopolisation. Corporatism and monopolisation is the enemy of capitalism in the sense of it being the right to go about your free establishment of business without hindrance. Small business owners will always suffer where corporations benefit, and in TTIP's case they benefit grossly. Small businesses will never be able to compete with their larger counterparts as a result of this deal, because they will lack the resources to take any kind of advantage of their liberties. Meanwhile corporations will benefit from the added advantage of TTIP. It will be even worse than the treatment Mr. Thoburn received over pounds and kilos.

Workers will not escape either. We will see much worse consequences for workers rights than we could ever imagine. The rights and liberties developed during the 18th and 19th century will be nothing more than words on a piece of paper. This is why it is so perplexing to me that the Labour Party and many of the Unions are still supporting European Union membership. I am quite sure it has nothing to do with the colossal funding they receive that goes to fattening the leaders' pay packets and promoting their pet causes -nothing to do with that at all! Remember, TTIP is an agreement with a country that has so far failed to recognise even the most basic of workers rights (at least by British standards) having accepted only two out of eight

ILO core labour standards. Imagine what it will be like to be a worker, toiling in an organisation that must survive under a corporatist dictatorship. Under a market where American corporations have assisted in the legislation and regulation, where such corporations can bring action in court against a government that doesn't side with them, and where these corporations are supported by the unelected and unaccountable European Union. A union, which, it seems, is not giving much thought to basic employment rights.

Do you think that all of the European Union directives and all of the Acts of Parliament in the world would be able to protect and save you? I am afraid to say that the only person who can protect you, and who has any vested interest in protecting you, is you. This is why it is important that you take notice of the legal implications that are being laid out before you here. In such circumstances losing your job may well be the lesser of all the potential evils, which is just as well considering Tufts University in the United States of America, published a study that suggested 600,000 jobs could be lost under TTIP's implementation[116]. This is without even mentioning the impact that it could have on the City of London, which as you now know is supposed to be protected under the Magna Carta, along with other cities. TTIP is more than just the pouring of acid onto the rights of workers and small businesses, it is the complete overhaul of our own constitutional arrangements and sovereignty in favour of multinational corporations, who along with the European Commission or those invested in the European dream, are the only ones who profit from it.

---

[116] Capaldo, Jeronim; *The Trans-Atlantic Trade and Investment Partnership: European Disintegration, Unemployment and Instability*, [October 2014], pages.2,4,15,19, Global Development and Environment Institute.

If this were coming directly from our own domestic government, we would not accept it. Part of the reason we are accepting TTIP is because it is being kept secret from us for the most part, which gives us practically nothing to oppose. We only know what we know from information that has been leaked, and similar arrangements that have been made with other countries. The critical difference being, if it were our own domestic government enacting this legislation, that we would be able to protect ourselves using the negative liberties bestowed upon us, we would be able to push them out of the seat of power with our electoral system, we would perhaps actually know what was going on in the first place. If we chose Brexit, we would be able to avoid this impending and almost irreversible disaster. Then from a position of independence, we could strike up our own trade deal with the USA and other countries, built on mutual terms that are in the United Kingdom's interests. At the moment, this deal is being done in the interests of the European Union elite, since trying to do it in the interests of 28 nations that cannot agree on the simplest of things and have different desires and needs, is impossible and unrealistic.

Molly Scott Cato MEP also claimed of TTIP:

> *"We hear much criticism of the "nanny state", but the world according to TTIP is more like Big Brother Corporation, where individual preferences are swept aside in the onward march of progress and order. It is the disturbing and unsettling worldview that David Korten envisaged in his 1995 book, When Corporations Rule the World. At the time the title seemed rhetorical; outlandish even. It seems considerably less so*

today [117]*."*

It is not often I would agree with a Green Party politician, but she is correct: TTIP is about a corporatist domination of Europe where you as an individual are dispensable. Notwithstanding this, TTIP's aims show another aim which is much more sinister. As you will remember from the Magna Carta, it reads: *"To no one will we sell, to no one deny or delay right or justice* [118]*."* Yet, when you reflect on TTIP, it is in direct contravention of this critical right of every citizen. Take into account the fact that TTIP allows wealthy corporations to help write law; to bring lawsuits against governments who do not legislate in its favour; and to take ownership of important public services. It is clear that the European Union are not striking a simple trade deal, they are selling liberty to corporations and denying liberty to the individual and the sovereign state. How can the Unions and the pro-EU lobby seriously claim that the European Union is an institution which supports the rights of workers when the same European Union is engaging in the sale of Europe, and the enslavement of every country and the liberty of each individual citizen in those countries with it?

---

[117] Cato, Molly Scott (In the Guardian), *'I've seen the secrets of TTIP, and it is built for corporations not citizens'*, [4th February 2015], Retrieved 2nd April 2016. - http://www.theguardian.com/commentisfree/2015/feb/04/secrets-ttip-corporations-not-citizens-transatlantic-trade-deal

[118] Article 40, *Magna Carta 1297* - http://www.bsswebsite.me.uk/History/MagnaCarta/magnacarta-1297.htm

Dominic Bardill

CHAPTER 12
THE NEGATIVES OF 'POSITIVE'

One of the biggest arguments, in terms of the law, that many people use to argue that Britain should remain in the European Union, is the Human Rights Argument.

> *"If Britain – a key member of the human rights council, a founding member of the UN and a privileged, permanent member of the security council – is considering a move that will potentially weaken a vital regional institution upholding fundamental human rights guarantees, this would be profoundly regrettable; damaging for victims and human rights protection; and contrary to this country's commendable history of global and regional engagement. Moreover, many other states, where civil society is currently threatened, may gleefully follow suit. Surely this is a legacy no British government would wish to inspire [119]."*
> *– Prince Zeid Ra'ad Al Hussein (Oct 2015)*

This is perhaps one of the lazier and less creative forms of scaremongering in the on-going European Union debate.

---

[119] The Independent; *'Scrapping the Human Rights Act will help protect human rights, Attorney General says'*, [25th February 2016], Retrieved 3rd March 2016 - http://www.independent.co.uk/news/uk/politics/scrapping-the-human-rights-act-will-help-protect-human-rights-attorney-general-says-a6894966.html

The idea that the United Kingdom, in all its malevolence and due to its inherent evil nature, will crush the weak and poor and cleanse everyone from its society that it does not want. Of course, it makes perfect sense that one of the leading nations in the abolition of slavery; giving women the vote; introducing the right to a fair trial and habeas corpus, effectively the home of liberty, must be kept in check by a mixture of recovering communist dictatorships, purveyors of war and oppressors of their own citizens. Yes, indeed, the European Union is the perfect candidate to ensure that the mother of modern liberty doesn't become a raving fascist, you know, that same raving fascist that she has never been before, but has, in the contexts of history, has faced from the very continent that is supposed to now police her.

Intellectually and legally lazy? Indeed! Incorrect? Absolutely! However, one could -and will, go even further. This is not merely an ignorance of the reality of things legally and constitutionally; it is not merely a misunderstanding or a misplaced appreciation for the rights of individuals. On the contrary, it is a deliberately misleading, fallacious and destructive piece of propaganda, which people living in the UK ought to grow wise to.

The Human Rights Act has been labelled as some to be the 'successor to the Magna Carta'. Ultimately, this is not completely wrong but it is misleading. It is correct to say that the Human Rights Act was drafted by British lawyers, moreover it is correct to say that the Human Rights Act embodies within it many of the liberties and principles that were developed in the Magna Carta centuries before. However, it is somewhat disingenuous to suggest that this automatically makes the Human Rights Act the natural successor to the Magna Carta and the subsequent principles of law that followed.

The Human Rights Act is the United Kingdom's implementation of the European Convention on Human Rights into United Kingdom law[120]. It provided a number of protections for the rights of United Kingdom citizens, in the sense that it placed a duty on the government to protect these rights and particularly to refrain from breaching or abusing them. The applicability of this law extends to any public body, which is defined in the act as one "whose functions are functions of a public nature". This means that any public body from the local council, through to the police, the courts and the government of the day, cannot act contrary to the rights laid out in the European Convention.

Nonetheless, was it really necessary in order to achieve the objective of protecting the rights of the citizen from abuse or contravention from the government? For example, the death penalty had been abolished in the United Kingdom since 1965; long before the United Kingdom introduced the Human Rights Act. Yet in Section 21 (5) of the Act we see that the death penalty is abolished. Furthermore, by virtue of our membership of the European Union, the United Kingdom was already bound by the European Convention; the difference with the introduction of the Human Rights Act being that claims were actionable in United Kingdom courts as opposed to the European Court of Human Rights in Strasbourg. In the interests of honesty, one must accept that this carries with it some positive as well as some negative effects.

---

[120] Human Rights Act 1998 - http://www.legislation.gov.uk/ukpga/1998/42/contents

One of the positives of the resulting legislation allowing action to be brought in the United Kingdom's Courts is quite simply the cost. Previously, those wishing to make a claim under the Human Rights Act had to spend enormous amounts of time, money and energy in taking their claim all the way to the Strasbourg court. It was a bureaucratic and expensive process that proved to be impractical for the most part. The introduction of the Human Rights Act meant that this was no longer necessary. In theory, this is a constructive thing; as someone who believes strongly in freedoms and liberty, I would be a hypocrite to suggest that increasing ease of access to justice was in some way a bad thing that should never be tolerated. Nevertheless, this positive is somewhat stumped when it is taken outside of its theoretical positivity and the practical implementation is given closer scrutiny.

The Human Rights Act's practical implications, like much of European Union law, differ vastly in terms of results, from the theory or professed values that underpin it. Firstly, and perhaps the most simple, is that it was completely and totally unnecessary. Certainly, for our continental friends the European Convention may well have been a necessary feature, after all we helped create it but didn't sign up to it for quite some time. The precise reason for this is because it was designed for the continent, not for the British. The British quite simply didn't need it, or anything even remotely similar to it! Given the fact that the United Kingdom invented liberty and exported it to much of the globe when the French were still trying to figure out which number republic they were on, it is laughable to suggest that this same nation requires the input of the far less qualified, and probably less intelligent judges, in the European Court of Human Rights.

The European Convention of Human Rights, which the Human Rights Act implements directly into English law, makes provisions for a number of rights and freedoms such as; the right to education; the right to a fair trial; the right not to be tortured or enslaved; freedom of speech, or conscience and with that freedom of religion[121]. It is important to note that the European Convention of Human Rights which takes the form of a treaty, is not strictly anything to do with the European Union per se, but rather it is a separate entity that is open to any signatory nation that wishes to sign it whether they are in the European Union or not. As a result, leaving the European Union would not necessarily mean rescinding our signature to the European Convention of Human Rights. Furthermore, even if we were to tear up the European Convention, the reason that Human Rights are law in the United Kingdom is that the Human Rights Act was passed by Act of Parliament. As a result, this statute would still remain.

The European Court of Human Rights has received much criticism for its often-absurd conclusions on certain matters. Lord Hoffman argued that the European Court of Human Rights was,

> "...unable to resist the temptation to aggrandise its jurisdiction and to impose uniform rules on Member States. It considers itself the equivalent of the Supreme Court of the United States, laying down a federal law of Europe".

This expression of frustration from Lord Hoffman, demonstrates that even though the Convention and the

---

[121] *European Convention on Human Rights*. (PDF FORMAT: http://www.echr.coe.int/Documents/Convention_ENG.pdf)

European Court of Human Rights are technically separate and distinct from the European Union, it is, as with most of the European Union law so far, very misleading. Lord Hoffman is suggesting that the European Court of Human Rights is partaking in the enforcement of a kind of federal Europe, which is something of an ambition for Europhiles. Interestingly, at present, the European Union is not actually bound by the European Convention of Human Rights and therefore cannot be held accountable by them, member states can still however be held accountable, even if they are doing something that the European Union has, by force of law, forced them to do. If this is not potentially some form of imprisonment of nations, placing them between a rock and a hard place, I do not know what is; one thing is for sure, the European Union and European Court of Human Rights appear very much to be working in tandem.

What we are seeing here is the perfect example of the types of liberties that were discussed in previous chapters. The Human Rights Act promotes the idea of positive liberty because it imposes state control over our liberties. The problem with this, as already mentioned, is that positive liberty places on the state a positive obligation to intervene, and this in turn places the control of rights into the hands of the state. With the negative liberties one would find in the Magna Carta, Charter of Liberties and Assize of Clarendon, we see that the state is only called to intervene where one's negative liberties are breached, and thus ultimately the point is for the state to stay out of the life of the individual, giving them full control of their own future.
To clarify further, take one of the rights that are supposedly protected under the Human Rights Act, for example Freedom of Conscience. This apparently guarantees that you are free to think as you wish; something that many

would agree is a fundamental right. The idea is that you should never be punished or penalised because of an opinion, belief, philosophy, and religion or thought that you hold. This is both practical and arguably moral, since if your mind is not free then ultimately your freedom cannot exist beyond it.

Nevertheless, in May 2014, LGBT activist Gareth Lee entered Ashers' Bakery in Belfast, where he placed an order for a cake that carried the words 'Support Gay Marriage'. Subsequently, Ashers' cancelled the order due to the fact that the owners of the bakers; Daniel and Amy McArthur, were devout Christians who did not agree with gay marriage. As a consequence, Mr Lee sued the bakery and won, which caused the bakery to pay him compensation. The judge in the case had declared that religion should have no place in determining the legal outcome of the case, and claimed that the bakers had discriminated against Mr Lee for being a homosexual[122].

The two bakers later went to the Court of Appeal to contest the judgment, but two days before the case was due to be heard the Attorney General intervened which caused a suspension on the proceedings according to the normal procedure. The Attorney General interceded in order to make a representation that the couple had, in his opinion, discriminated against Mr Lee. The intervention did not destroy the possibility of an appeal, but it unnecessarily delay it[123]. The premise of the appeal as far as Human

---

122 The Guardian; *'Northern Ireland bakers guilty of discrimination over gay marriage cake'*, [19th May 2015], Retrieved 30th May 2015 -
http://www.theguardian.com/society/2015/may/19/northern-ireland-ashers-baking-company-guilty-discrimination-gay-marriage-cake
123 Belfast Telegraph; *'Ashers bakery appeal: Northern Ireland's Attorney General gets green light for involvement in 'gay cake' case'*, [3rd March 2016].

Rights law was that the previous judge's ruling was a breach of the McArthur's freedom of conscience, and it proved to be a hot topic for debate. So, let us look at the question of freedom of conscience in this example, from the perspective of positive liberty (the European Union and European Convention's way of regarding liberty), and negative liberty (the proper, British way of regarding liberty), and see what the results and implications are, was the ruling a breach of their Human Rights?

From a Positive Liberty perspective

As we now know, the Human Rights Act take the position of positive liberty, and so this is the position that the original judge would have been taking when she declared that discrimination had taken place and that the McArthur's were not free to allow their religion to interfere with their business. As a result, in refusing to bake the cake they had discriminated against Mr Lee and thus the state was obliged to intervene in order to uphold the rights of the Mr Lee. If you will recall, positive liberty gives you the *freedom to* something, and so they were upholding his freedom to buy a cake. Due to the fact that this is not a naturally occurring situation, but rather it is a manufactured viewpoint because it places the arbitration of rights directly into the hands of the state, the state determined that Mr Lee's right to a cake was more important than the Christian couple's right to refuse service. Naturally, Mr Lee's right to a cake, will be portrayed as his right not to be discriminated against.

This stance is ultimately full of holes. Firstly, the Christian couple would have had no idea that Mr Lee himself was a homosexual, and therefore could not have logically been discriminating against him. What the couple were objecting to is the message that was on the cake. They were not preventing him from having a cake; they were simply making use of their right not to be forced to make it. Positive liberty doesn't care about this, and so the result is two fold. Firstly, just as I stated before regarding positive liberty bestowing rights not on the individual, but on the state, who then decides which rights are to be granted to the individual, and when to impart them, the same is true here. What you may see at first glance, is a case of some mean and horrible Christians trampling over the rights of a poor, innocent, meek LGBT activist who in no way targeted the bakery because it was run by Christians, honest. If you scratch the surface, and dig a little deeper though, you will find that in actual fact positive liberty ends up being completely political, driven by whatever agenda is fashionable and trendy at the time. It does not, therefore, deal in absolutes; by its very nature it is regularly reviewed and renewed, which is another way of saying that it changes. In this instance, the non-existent right of Mr Lee took precedence over the actual freeborn rights of Mr and Mrs McArthur.

This is nothing to do with what your opinions on gay marriage or homosexuality are. This is purely a matter of principle; a question of whether liberty is a universal and intrinsic thing that exists eternally, outside of manmade structures. The issue with positive liberty is that it becomes morally relative, and indeed politically relative. When we examine the repercussion of the judgment against the bakery, we see that the right of individuals to think as they wish, and the right of individuals to go about their private business as they please, are not the only things under threat. Indeed, as I stated before, positive liberty grants rights to the state, and as a result of this judgment those rights that the state possess clearly extend to the rights of the state to force you against your conscience, to intervene in your private business, and perhaps worst of all, to compel you to act against your will. More specifically, Peter Hitchens notes that this judgment even has repercussions outside of the religious or LGBT sphere;

> *'Imagine if 'The Guardian' could be forced by law to publish a column by me. If you think that ludicrous, then you must say the same of this judgement, with its wholly mistaken concentration on the sale of the cake, and its apparent inability to see the role of the bakers as publishers* [124]*."*

He is correct. if the state can penalise you for *not* publishing a written message on a cake, imagine what they can publish newspapers and the media for *not* writing or publishing? Positive liberty once again, favours and empowers the state above all, and allows the state to disable or enable whomever it sees fit based on its own agenda and desires, or the fashions of the time. This is not true liberty; it is rather a cheapened, faux-liberty that we should all collectively and individually reject. Indeed, the infamous LGBT rights activist Peter Tatchell surprised everybody when he came forward not in support of Mr Lee's blatant provocation, but rather in favour of the Christian bakers;

> *"... the court erred by ruling that Lee was discriminated against because of his sexual orientation and political opinions. His cake request was refused not because he was gay, but because of the message he asked for. There is no*

---

[124] Hitchens, Peter; *'Peter Tatchell (again) is Right. The 'Gay Cake' case is about liberty, not discrimination'*, 1st February 2016, Mail Online.

evidence that his sexuality was the reason Ashers declined his order[125]."

Indeed he identifies exactly the problem. Imagine for a moment if a heterosexual went to a bakery owned and run by a homosexual couple that believed strongly in sexual liberation and same sex marriage. Imagine if they had asked the bakers to bake a cake containing the message 'Homosexuality is a evil' or 'Gay marriage is wrong', or even 'Support Traditional Marriage'. In such a situation, the bakers do not know for a fact that the person asking for the cake is heterosexual, and this would not be their motivation in refusing to bake the cake if they chose not to. No, they might refuse to bake the cake, and it would be because the message they are being asked to publish on the cake goes against their conscience and judgment. If they did refuse, should they face a lawsuit? Of course not. They should be fully entitled to refuse private business to anyone they wish, the law should not be a tool for the state to compel you to do things as positive liberty allows the state to do. Rather, the law should protect the baker from being forced against their conscience by not allowing the other party to force them, and should protect the other party by allowing them to go and seek other business elsewhere. The fact is, and we of course know this full well, that if an LGBT baker refused service in such circumstances, there would be no outcry and no lawsuit, because as I mentioned before, this positive liberty approach allows the state to be the arbitrator and thus populism and fashion take higher importance. The state would treat a homosexual baker

---

[125] Tatchell, Peter; *'I've changed my mind on the gay cake row. Here's why,'* [1st February 2016], The Guardian, Retrieved 3rd May 2016 -
http://www.theguardian.com/commentisfree/2016/feb/01/gay-cake-row-i-changed-my-mind-ashers-bakery-freedom-of-conscience-religion

entirely different because of the current fashions and political agendas.

This is the danger of positive liberty and this is why the McArthurs have been treated so horrendously. You do not have a right to have a cake baked by a particular person, that is not a liberty. You do have the right or liberty to seek someone who will bake it, do business with them, and not be hindered from it. You do not have the right to force someone to do business with you or penalise them for not, and certainly not when it goes against their conscience.

From a Negative Liberty perspective

The actual bakery incident wasn't a Human Rights claim on the part of Mr Lee, this was a matter of discrimination. The Human Rights issue enters into the debate with the appeal of the Christian bakers. As we know, from the perspective of negative liberty and traditionally in the excellent approach of English law historically, you have freedom of conscience and thought. The Human Rights Act purports to enshrine that. However, the difference between the two is that one takes the approach of positive liberty, the other takes the negative liberty approach, which is, as you will see, a much fairer approach which may not always grant your personal desired outcome. As already established, the problem that the Human Rights Act places rights into the hands of the state because it supports the positive liberty view. So how would negative liberty work in these circumstances?

Well, it would be very simple. The owner of the bakery has freedom of conscience and the freedom to practice his private business without whomever he chooses unhindered by the state. Whilst the LGBT activist has the right to his opinions on homosexual marriage and live his own life according to his sexuality, views or anything else he so chooses. When the LGBT activist asks for a cake supporting his own views to be made, the baker has the right to refuse service. The LGBT activist does not have the right to a cake, whilst it is his freedom to buy a cake, it is not his freedom to buy a cake from that particular bakery. Consequently, the baker may refuse, and the activist or any other customer may take their business elsewhere to one of probably hundreds if not thousands of bakeries that will carry out his request. In this circumstance, neither the baker nor the LGBT activist have had their rights, liberties or freedoms infringed and the state has absolutely no requirement to act. This, is liberty. It may not always obey your own personal political, moral or social views, but it is liberty. The point we should be focusing on in this instance is the underlying principle, which is liberty and freedom itself.

Whilst in one instance you may think the baker should bake the cake, the fact is that true, negative liberty dictates that he should not be forced. Why is this important? Well, it means that you too cannot be forced. Picture a future where a government or state were to take over which sympathised with a set of values that you viewed as abhorrent and dangerous; the position of positive liberty, by granting rights to the state, would support the state in forcing you to obey those values even in your own private affairs. Consequently, we must uphold the principle of negative liberty and freedom of conscience, to protect all of us, because whilst one day infringing on it may make you happy, another day you may find yourself in quite the opposite situation.

The Human Rights Act however, failed to do anything to protect the right that it supposedly supports –freedom of conscience or freedom of religion. Why? Because as already pointed out, it rests on the idea of positive liberty, and thus it is up to the State to Act. The United Kingdom's courts need only 'consider' the rulings of the European Court of Human Rights, and thus your own liberties and rights under this Act are in actual fact protected as far as the state wishes to protect them. In the case of this bakery, their ideology did not fit the fashion, and so the Human Rights Act has so far done nothing for them simply because the state has done nothing for them. This is another example of positive liberty, and in this case the Human Rights Act, ultimately granting power to a state that is not swayed by principle but by its own agenda and the trends of the time. It is, by all standards, unacceptable and dangerous.

CHAPTER 13
WHO KNOWS WHERE THE BODY IS?

Another example of where the Human Rights Act has proved completely ineffective, as well as where negative liberty and indeed the traditional and precious freedoms we are supposed to possess have been trampled on, is the European Arrest Warrant.

Andrew Christopher Symeou was accused of murdering Jonathan Hiles in Cyprus, something that he denied from the outset. In 2009, Symeou was subsequently extradited to Greece where his world was turned upside down and he travelled a perilous path of misery, uncertainty and pain, in circumstances that most decent, liberty-loving people would never wish, even upon their fiercest enemies.

The case against Symeou was completely fabricated – essentially framing him for a crime he had not committed. Friends of his had identified Symeou in photographs. One of the questionable elements of this was the fact that in the photographs that were shown to the witnesses, Symeou had been circled next to the word 'perpetrator'; clearly a flagrant attempt by the authorities to encourage those witnesses to identify him. Additionally, all of the witness statements contained more or less identical words, structure and vocabulary. One might usually expect this to be the case, indicating perhaps that the accounts are true because they corroborate. Nevertheless, to have statements that are taken in different places, at different times and on different days, give such physically and literally parallel versions, is suspicious and unusual. Interestingly, two witnesses that signed to implicate Symeou, retracted their statements as soon as they were out of police custody, claiming that the police used brutality to force them to adhere to their chosen route. An account, reported in the Daily Telegraph, quotes one of those very witnesses as saying:

> *"I told [the Greek police officer] that I didn't see Andrew Symeou get no one and he was saying 'Really?' three times, and then I said no again. I got hit by the big guy with a fist quite hard. The big guy left the room and came back with a black police bat and was tapping it in his hand. I couldn't think, I was just sitting there waiting to be hit* [126].*"*

The allegations from these witnesses that they had been forced by police under duress, with the use of violence and intimidation, to testify against Symeou was further supported by Georgina Clay. Georgina, had seen them both after they left police custody, battered, bruised and badly beaten. To further add fuel to the flames of doubt that consistently grew regarding Symeou's involvement in the murder, further investigations were done by the inquest that took place in Wales, into the death of Jonathan. The witnesses who had maintained testimonies against Symeou failed to give any accurate description of him to the

---

[126] Gilligan, Andrew; *Extradition nightmare: 'When we first saw our son in jail it broke our hearts',* [21st August 2010]. The Daily Telegraph.

inquest, and drastically changed important and obvious elements of their stories.

Andrew Symeou spent a total of one whole year in some of the worst prisons in Greece. He and his parents reported that he would be abused, taunted and bullied by prison guards, who would verbally harass him for being English, and would vandalise his belongings before he was transferred to new prisons. Symeou would have to sleep with cockroaches falling onto him and crawling over him at night, could not wash or eat properly, and slept on a concrete bed in sweltering heat and unsanitary conditions. All of this, and worse, happened to an innocent man, in the 21st Century, in a country in Europe, and there was absolutely nothing that the United Kingdom could do to protect him. The following account is taken from a journal kept by Mr. Symeou during his stay in a Greek prison. It paints a picture of almost mediaeval conditions, and it is worth reflecting on as if it were oneself, or worse, a member of one's family, in light of his innocence.

"I can't believe it's been 300 days tomorrow. I'm fed up of not being free. I'm fed up of it all. I'm fed up of Tupperware containers and plastic cutlery. I'm fed up of food coupons and squatting to shit at specific times. I'm fed up of living in a cell with heroin-addicted thieves. I'm fed up of living out of a sports bag. I'm fed up of having no privacy. I'm fed up of dirty showers. I'm fed up of phone cards. I'm fed up of seeing my family through a dirty window for half an hour. I'm fed up with hearing Greek. I'm fed up of Greece. I'm fed up of being locked up. I'm fed up of eating shit prison food full of spit and bogeys. I'm fed up of sleeping on a one-inch-thick mattress. I'm fed up of being wrongly accused of killing someone. I'm fed up of not being happy. I'm fed up of having a headache. I'm

fed up of having to write in this stupid fucking journal like a 12-year-old girl. I'm fed up of having anxiety. I'm fed up of everything [...] Ok I think I've established that I'm fed up. I feel so frickin' weak because I can never let my guard down; it's exhausting. I'm tired; I want to be free again. I don't deserve this shit [127] *."*

It was situations like this, that England created concepts and principles such as Habeas Corpus, precisely to prevent. Yet centuries on, at a time when we all arrogantly convince ourselves that we are so much more civilised and enlightened than our forefathers, this very incident is happening to an innocent Briton, as well as people of other nationalities, and our own governments not only fail to intervene, but they actively sign up to it. Why couldn't the United Kingdom do anything to protect Mr. Symeou? After all, most reasonable people would agree that a Government has a duty to protect its citizens from harm. The Deputy Prime Minister at the time, Nick Clegg, even commented on how unacceptable Mr. Symeou's treatment had been;

"No-one should ever have to go through what Andrew and the Symeou family went through. It was a travesty that they were made to suffer so much for so long. His case showed that there were real problems with the way the EAW was operating and that things needed to change as a result [128] *."*

Whilst it is all well and good for the Deputy Prime Minister

---

[127] Symeou, Andrew; *'Extradited: The European Arrest Warrant and My Fight for Justice from a Greek Prison Cell'*, Journal extract – Day 299 – 15 May 2010, 12th May 2015, Biteback Publishing.

[128] Clegg, Nick; The Independent; *'Nick Clegg: Nigel Farage has modern justice –and my position on Andrew Symeou – all wrong'*, 27th March 2014.

to complain about Mr. Symeou's treatment, it is not exactly sufficient. The United Kingdom should have prevented the extradition of Symeou unless certain agreements were made to ensure his fair treatment, which the United Kingdom's government should have supervised along with assurances of a fair trial. Sadly though, whether the United Kingdom Government was convinced that Mr. Symeou's trial was going to be fair or his treatment was going to be humane, or not, is irrelevant. The British Judge in the case clarified the situation aptly when he declared that there was no remit for him to intervene, saying *"The abuse jurisdiction of [Britain] does not extend to considering misconduct or bad faith by the police of [Greece]*[129].*"* To clarify then, the practicalities of the warrant were such that whilst the warrant issued by Greece extended across the borders to the United Kingdom, the ability of the United Kingdom to uphold the liberties of, and protect, her people, did not extend across the borders to Greece. If Mr. Symeou were due to be extradited to a country outside of the EU however, then the United Kingdom would have some capacity to intervene in some way. Ultimately, the European Arrest Warrant strips the home state of any power to defend its people, and simultaneously empowers a foreign state to exercise jurisdiction over said individual. It is fundamentally absurd then, that a less developed European Union member state can extend its arm so far into Britain's legal system in a way that a more advanced non-EU country would never conceivably be allowed. Any criminal justice tool, which empowers a foreign body to such an extent that an entire foreign state may target a citizen in his own country, whilst anaesthetising the home state of that individual, is

---

[129] Gilligan, Andrew; *Extradition nightmare: 'When we first saw our son in jail it broke our hearts'*, [21st August 2010]. The Daily Telegraph.

dictatorial and authoritarian. It is a danger to the liberties of the individual because it allows foreign states to essentially declare war on the small man, which is ultimately a danger to us all.

Mr. Symeou himself condemned the extradition laws and cried out for justice in the future; *"British courts did not have the discretion to prevent my extradition... I want to stop this happening to other innocent people* [130]*."* In that sentence alone, Mr. Symeou nails the problem down cleanly and clearly. The problem is that the European Arrest Warrant removes any jurisdiction of our own national courts over our own people, or people living here. The effect of the European Arrest Warrant in allowing countries with a far inferior judicial and criminal justice system to simply pluck citizens from their homes here in the United Kingdom, transport them to foreign countries, and subject them to objectively inhumane treatment is in itself an injustice. There is perhaps no more blatant a way to breach someone's freeborn liberties, than to override Habeas Corpus with what is essentially a watered down, fast-track version, of the standard International Law extradition process.

There are a number of countries in the world that have a policy of not extraditing their citizens to certain foreign jurisdictions. In fact, most countries in the world don't have any extradition treaties signed that gives rise to some kind of automatic extradition rights to foreign countries to take citizens from their own countries. This is clearly an immensely sensible position from the point of view of someone who values not only the freedom and liberty of the individual, but the concept of the rule of law, the right

---

[130] Hislop, Leah; *'Andrew Symeou criticizes extradition laws'*, [2nd November 2011], The Daily Telegraph.

to a fair trial and Habeas Corpus. In instances where there are some extradition treaties, you will find that such treaties exist between countries that have some kind of alliance, or where the government of each country recognises that their counterpart maintains the same legal and humanitarian standards that they do. For example, the USA has extradition treaties with the United Kingdom[131], but it does not have extradition treaties with Afghanistan or Iraq. This is clearly for obvious reasons. Whilst nobody can claim that the USA is the perfect bastion of liberty and freedom, or fairness in their judicial system; they have a far more similar standard and outlook to the United Kingdom, than Saudi Arabia does. The whole principle, is based on the idea that the government should aim to protect its citizens from being subject to maltreatment manifest in nations with judicial activism, unfair and inhumane practices, and corrupt criminal justice systems. One would even go further and suggest that government's first duty should be to the citizen, controversial right? Well actually, if one reflects, it is clear that such a position is far from extreme or controversial. The precedent in the UK of presumed innocence, the right to a fair trial and habeas corpus, should always be of paramount importance to the Government that has inherited the heavy burden of upholding such values. They have absolutely no business signing away or surrendering such responsibilities to countries that have consistently failed to uphold them; yet this is exactly what they have done.

The European Arrest Warrant sought to 'streamline' extraditions between EU Member States. It is important to note that as history has taught us, big governments wishing to 'streamline' things does not usually mean good news for

---

131 Extradition Act 2003 -http://www.legislation.gov.uk/ukpga/2003/41/contents

the small man on the street; the European Arrest Warrant was no different. What did the streamlines entail? What was the purpose of streamlining? Well, it was quite simply to make is easier to extradite people from country to country. In fact, in EU Law it is easier to extradite and transport a human being, who is merely accused of a crime, away from home and across the continent, than it is to transport a truckload of lambs on their way to an abattoir. Ponder on that for a moment.

Under normal extradition law, a nation-state has various rights and powers in the extradition proceedings. For example, a nation could well refuse to surrender a citizen and many do –particularly to countries that are the home of judicial and criminal justice systems that are brutal or corrupt. In addition to the right of a country to refuse to surrender its citizens, nations also hold bargaining power in extradition proceedings. Diplomats play an enormous role and allow nations to make certain demands on the nation that has filed for extradition, which could and often does involve demands regarding the treatment of the suspect. The use of the term suspect is exceptionally important, because the European Arrest Warrant seems to impliedly deny this absolutely vital tenet of justice; one, that has been established, comes from our own nation. What ought to happen, is a country should itself investigate into the likelihood of their citizen having committed any crime, through the exchange of evidence and information between the two countries. The country should then look at whether there is the likelihood of humane treatment and a fair trial, if there isn't, then their citizen should never be handed over. How can a nation, or a government, claim to believe in fair trials and humane treatment if they themselves deny the presumption of innocence, by signing up to authoritarian tools like the European Arrest Warrant? In doing so, they pre-emptively sign away the most basic and absolutely vital liberties that belong to their population.

One shouldn't pretend to be surprised by this however. Whilst Nick Clegg himself publicly condemned the treatment of Andrew Symeou, he would not go so far as to uphold the ancient liberties that this country pioneered and exported to the world. Instead, he did quite the opposite. Favouring the Brussels dogma, Mr. Clegg went on to pour scorn on the idea of ancient freedoms and liberties that are still very much grounded in English law, even if they are frequently trampled on. After a debate with Nigel Farage, Mr. Clegg wrote:

> *"In the debate I held with Nigel Farage last night, he made a series of false claims about the European Arrest Warrant (EAW), which is the agreement that allows us to fast-track the extradition of suspects between the countries of the EU. He said he would prefer to rely on historical extradition treaties stretching all the way back to the year 1174 [132]."*

A 'liberal' democrat who dismisses any real idea of liberty, lovingly handmade in Britain, in favour of EU legislation that has been shown to directly undermine the principles of fair trials, habeas corpus, humane treatment, the rule of law and the presumption of innocence. Perhaps Mr. Clegg despises these important principles so much because they too date back too many centuries. Naturally, because something is old, it must be 'outdated' and worthy of scorn. Whilst anything modern, new and shiny, is automatically good. Right? One can only assume that Mr. Clegg's 'age-discrimination' towards old extradition treaties, in the face

---

[132] Clegg, Nick; The Independent; *'Nick Clegg: Nigel Farage has modern justice –and my position on Andrew Symeou – all wrong'*, 27th March 2014.

of evidence that the current model is an anathema, is born out of his deep-seated hatred for his own country and heritage. Seemingly, just like those treaties are bad because they are old, which is not really an argument, so too must all of the principles underpinning freedom and liberty be automatically bad —because they're old. It is arguable that Mr. Clegg's loathing for these important assets, may not be because he hates justice, but rather that he loves the EU Project far more.

A self-professed liberal who denies liberty, is little more than a democrat who denies people the vote, and yet sadly, his viewpoint is acceptable to some people, somewhere. The point remains however, that it shouldn't be acceptable to anyone who wishes to preserve true freedom and liberty, within a respectable and reliable legal structure. Mr. Clegg goes on to write:

> *"We've changed the rules so that no-one will be extradited unless there is a clear intention on the part of the receiving country to bring the case to trial. That will mean people in Andrew's situation won't have to sit in jail for months waiting while their case is still being investigated. We have also legislated for a proportionality test, which will mean that our courts are able to consider whether extradition would have a disproportionate impact on the fundamental rights of the person who is being requested for extradition. And we will allow for video-conferencing to be used so that people can be questioned from abroad without leaving the UK [133]."*

This is of course a complete fabrication of the truth, which would hardly come as any real surprise given our experience of Mr. Clegg over the years. For instance, Mr.

---

[133] ^Ibid

Clegg claims that we have effected some kind of change in the rules, yet not only is there no evidence that this has actually happened, it is also impossible that it ever could happen. The European Arrest Warrant is dictated down from the top as a result of the terms of the Maastricht Treaty. Member states, or any party to any treaty for that matter, do not have the jurisdiction, power or ability to change its terms after it has been signed. The way that the European Arrest Warrant works in practice is that one member state files the warrant –usually by court order, and the other member state hands over their citizens. It really is as simple as that. Indeed, there are conditions that member states can lay down, as well as circumstances where the warrant may not be executed, but nevertheless there is no procedure or capacity for a member state to outright refuse.

Cases where surrender **must not** be granted are situations such as; where it concerns an offence that is part of an amnesty; where the suspect has been acquitted, convicted and already served a sentence in any member state for the same offence; or where the suspect is below the age of criminal responsibility in the executing state. Additionally, there are instances where surrender **may not** be granted, or may be refused by the home state of the accused. These situations are; where there is already a prosecution underway for the same offence; where the executing state's authorities have decided not to prosecute; where the prosecution has already reached final judgment; where the offence actually falls under the jurisdiction of the home state of the accused and statute would not permit a prosecution (statute barred); where the accused has already been tried in a third country and a final judgment made; the offence was actually committed in the accused's home state; or where the offence has taken place outside of the issuing state and the executing state would not permit a prosecution of that offence outside of its own territory.

Suffice to say, contrary to Mr. Clegg's claims quoted above, there is nothing in either the mandatory grounds for refusal, nor in the optional grounds, that provide any substance for a country to refuse to execute a warrant based on concerns regarding the treatment of their citizens, or on a fair trial. The reality is that the European Union are not concerned with this, and do not wish to pay it any serious credence. In fact, the European Union has even managed to expressly dismiss, in advance, any possibility of a country raising any sufficient or justified concerns regarding the judicial system and criminal proceedings of another member state, in relation to the execution of a European Arrest Warrant. In European law, each member state *"must be regarded as capable of providing sufficient minimum safeguards for a fair trial in a civilised country[134]"*. In other words, you do not have a choice. If you are legitimately concerned about the safeguards in place to protect one of your citizens, then that is just tough luck.

There have, allegedly, been some attempts to provide some safeguards for those who are the subject of extradition under the EAW. The European Council of Ministers made some amendments, recognising the need for *"enhancing the procedural rights of persons and fostering the application of the principle of mutual recognition to decisions rendered in the absence of the person concerned at the trial [135]"*. The 2009 amendments are

---

[134] Gilligan, Andrew; *Extradition nightmare: 'When we first saw our son in jail it broke our hearts'*, [21st August 2010]. The Daily Telegraph.
[135] Council Framework Decision 2009/299/JHA of 26 February 2009.

most likely the glorious and benevolent changes to which Mr. Clegg was referring, if you will excuse my sarcasm and cynicism. The amendments provided grounds for a refusal to execute a warrant when; the accused was summonsed in person, or not summonsed in person and failed to attend the trial whilst knowing the time and place of it; where the accused knew the details of trial and instructed lawyers to defend them; where the accused received a judgment and did not appeal for any reason; or where they may appeal or demand a retrial upon surrendering. If these were the changes that Mr. Clegg was eluding too, then once again they fail to address any of the very real aforementioned problems inherent in the EU extradition system, not least because they only apply to trial *in absentia*, or in other words when the accused is tried in their absence. It is completely unrelated to situations like that of Andrew Symeou, and in no way attempts to address the inequity and injustice in the emasculation of superior judicial systems and the empowerment of inferior ones. That could perhaps be why Mr. Clegg merely mentions some vague changes without providing any real evidence or detail for them, which only further demonstrates how the modern political class have begun to hold British-born principles in utter contempt.

Habeas Corpus translates roughly to 'You shall have the body', which essentially pertains to the idea that nobody shall be held or imprisoned without evidence, in other words, a 'body' of evidence. It is an integral part of the UK Constitution because it is this convention that prevents tyranny of the state against the individual in its most raw form. That is, the ability of a government or the state, to take you and place you in prison for absolutely no reason. It rests on the fundamental principle of the presumption of innocence, which is that one is *'innocent until proven guilty'* or as the Latin expression goes; *'Ei incumbit probatio qui dicit, non qui negat'* (the burden of proof is on the one who accuses, not the one who denies). This principle, once again, was pioneered by England, whilst many other nations had no such grasp of the concept.

By modern standards though, it may sound like a ridiculous concept; what government in the 21st century would ever dare to imprison its own citizens without any justification or charge against them? Ridiculous a concept it may be to you and I, in our ignorance, nevertheless the fact of the matter is that this is not just something that took place centuries ago in an age different to our own; thousands of people across the world are imprisoned without charge across the globe. In fact, some of the countries that engage in this practice may well surprise you.

The International Centre for Prison Studies published a number of interesting findings in their 'World Pre-trial/Remand Imprisonment List (WPTRIL)', which was published in June 2014. I suspect the numbers in 2016 are not wholly different, therefore using this as a basis to go on, we can gauge some idea as to just how common imprisonment without trial is in the world, and what type of countries are likely to engage in it. It is important to note that in the WPTRIL's list, the focus, or measure, is based on people who are held on remand, or 'pre-trial'. When someone is held on remand or in pre-trial imprisonment, it essentially means that they are put in prison or held in custody before their trial or without a trial on the basis that their situation has met the respective criteria (dependent on the law of the country) to be held in such a way. Someone may be held on remand for example, if they are likely to try to escape the country when granted bail, or when the nature of the crime they are charged with is exceptionally dangerous and serious so that it might be in the public interest to restrain their freedoms pending trial. The problem with this is of course that there is a difficult balancing act between keeping the population safe, whilst respecting the liberties and freedoms of the individual.

The findings of the report, claim that in 56% of countries, there is a range from 10% and 40% of the prison population who are 'pre-trial' prisoners, or prisoners on remand[136]. If one focuses on countries with the highest proportion, relative to prison population, then we find ourselves looking at parts of Africa, parts the Americas and various areas of Asia –particularly the South Central and Western parts of Asia. In these areas of the world, the proportion of prisoners who are 'pre-trial', represent 40%[137]. What does this say about 'pre-trial' imprisonment? In one sense, it suggests that in those countries in continents that are, to say the least, far from bastions of civil liberties and individual rights, there is a higher tendency to use 'pre-trial' imprisonment. However, on the other hand, with regards to this limited statistical information, it could also be perfectly fair to argue that it simply represents criminal trends of the respective countries. Naturally, there are at times quite sensible reasons to keep someone in prison before trial. For example, in crimes of particular danger to society, such as a suspected terrorist or someone known to have links to an organisation, who may have connections that might try to help him escape. Or a persistent offender, where the risk of releasing the individual might outweigh the arguments for

---

[136] International Centre for Prison Studies; *World Pre-trial/Remand Imprisonment List (Second Edition)*, 18th June 2014.
[137] ^Ibid

it. Consequently, it can quite easily be suggested, without further evidence to prove otherwise, that those countries using pre-trial imprisonment the most are those countries that may possibly have higher political, or violent crime rates, and that there is a justification for this. It is difficult to really know for sure, without further investigation.

Of course it would be wholly unrealistic for anyone to pretend that there is never a conflict between liberty and security. As a matter of fact, one would suggest that liberty and security are the two biggest rivals of all the political and social concepts that exist. No two principles have ever been more at loggerheads than these two. I think of them somewhat as siblings in a fierce rivalry; on the one hand there is liberty, that freethinking and expressive –almost youthful sibling, who wishes to break away and do its own thing, make its own life and carve its own path. Yet at times, it can find itself in trouble, and making the kind of decisions that render it vulnerable, fragile and in dire straits. On the other side, there is security; the stay at home sibling, who doesn't like to venture too far astray and is always extremely careful and thorough in its approach, whilst at times finding itself restrained to the extent so as to be ineffective or counterproductive –even obstructive. The two siblings are locked in a bitter sibling rivalry, at odds and yet strangely complimentary to each other. Without liberty, there cannot truly be any real security, yet without some measure of security, one cannot truly take advantage of liberty.

It is of course difficult to know exactly how many people are held in the world's prisons without trial. Not least because the nature of those countries that partake in such activities is such that they are unlikely to declare it so publicly. Usually, people who are held without trial or charge are people who are held for political or social reasons. This is usually the case with countries like North Korea, who are insular, secretive and isolated states. Consequently, it is almost impossible to calculate how many people in North Korea or similar secretive states are held without charge or trial. One would suggest however, that it isn't unreasonable to assume that it is a rather high number.

The United Kingdom of course has her fair share of prisoners held pre-trial or on remand. Naturally, as one has already stated, there is sometimes good reason for doing this. At the time of writing, about 9.3% of pre-trial prisoners in England and Wales are untried, which represents a much smaller percentage than the average in the world, and one of the lowest in the European Union[138]. This is because it is far less likely in the United Kingdom that someone who is merely accused of a crime is going to be placed in a jail cell until the justice system can get around to a trial. Unless the suspect is known, and dangerous, the English legal system would not allow it. So why would we hand over, a British citizen, without any evidence, to a foreign jurisdiction with a pre-trial detainee rate that is double or triple the size of our own? We do not unnecessarily imprison people because Habeas Corpus is still very relevant in the United Kingdom and remains an integral part of English law, even without many Brits ever having heard of Habeas Corpus. The fact is that evidential trials, as we learned when discussing the previous constitutional documents, came from this country. We introduced trial by jury based on evidence, whilst many countries were simply cutting off people's heads at the drop

---

[138] ^Ibid

of an accusation. Habeas Corpus requires evidence, to imprison someone, it means 'You should have the body" as in the *body* of evidence. If you do not, then the accused should be, and always will be, free to go. Exactly as it should be in fact.

The European Arrest Warrant then, is a direct contradiction of the Habeas Corpus, since it allows United Kingdom citizens to be simply plucked from their homes and sent to a foreign country where they may, or may not stand trial and will be held in conditions that we would not even place the worst serial killer. There have even been situations where Arrest Warrants have been issued for minor offences, including traffic offences. Nevertheless, regardless of the offence, the principle is that it is unacceptable for a British citizen to be handed over to a jurisdiction, without any evidence, that is inferior in quality and does not share the same outlook, as our own.

It took the United Kingdom several years to extradite the Islamist Abu Quatada to Jordan, due to fears of Human Rights violations and thus rulings from the European Court of Human Rights. Yet, Mr. Symeou, and others, have been transported at the flick of a pen, to foreign countries to face horrific environments, on frivolous and often fabricated claims. The United Kingdom's government has not protected them, because it cannot protect them, and the European Union is complicit. What more can we expect when we sign ourselves up to an organisation that replaces our negative freeborn liberties, such as Habeas Corpus, with positive liberties where you are chained until the state unchains you as it sees fit? Our own politicians such as David Cameron and Nick Clegg may well like the idea of handing their citizens over to the European Union to be dealt with, but isn't it a sad day when a document from 1297 has a better concept of how the individual should be treated by the state, than a politician of the 21st century, remember?...

> "No free man shall be seized or imprisoned, or stripped of his rights or possessions, or outlawed or exiled, or deprived of his standing in any other way, nor will we proceed with force against him, or send others to do so, except by the lawful judgement of his equals or by the law of the land [139].

> "To no one will we sell, to no one deny or delay right or justice. No free man shall be seized or imprisoned, or stripped of his rights or possessions, or outlawed or exiled . nor will we proceed with force against him . Except by the lawful judgement of his equals or by the law of the land [140]. "

How is the European Arrest Warrant not a complete desecration of these important liberties that were recognised in the Magna Carta so many centuries ago? The answer is, it is nothing less than a desecration. Moreover, how has the Human Rights Act done itself justice by intervening in its place? The answer is, it hasn't, and indeed it has categorically proven to be exactly what it really is; the kind of illusion of freedom that actually sides with the state, which is always the case with positive liberty.

Even more recently we have seen examples of the contempt that the European Union, or those 'great minds' behind it, have for the individual. A German comedian recently mocked the Turkish leader Erdogan on television; he probably did not expect that his own leader, Angela

---

[139] Article 39, *Magna Carta 1297* -
http://www.bsswebsite.me.uk/History/MagnaCarta/magnacarta-1297.htm
[140] Article 40, *Magna Carta 1297* -
http://www.bsswebsite.me.uk/History/MagnaCarta/magnacarta-1297.htm

Merkel, would allow his prosecution after Erdogan demanded it. That's right -a German comedian, prosecuted in his own country, for mocking the leader of Turkey[141]. How long before Cameron approves of the arrest of some of our best loved comedians, for making fun of Merkel? I suspect not long with the direction the European Union is heading. Why would Merkel do this to her own countryman? After she brazenly marched with *JeSuisCharlie*? Perhaps it is so Turkey would take some migrants back? Or perhaps it was to sweeten Turkey up for their impending entry into the European Union, after which we will share a border with Syria. One thing is for sure, if a comedian can be arrested in the European Union, with no protection under the beloved Human Rights Act and with the support of his own leader, then it is an assault on freedom of thought, conscience and expression; all important liberties of the individual. Oh, and by the way, just to stand in solidarity with *Jan Böhmermann*, the arrested comedian, I'll just say this: Erdogan, is a complete moron — indeed he is a joke of a man!

So, as we await my impending arrest, we must consider the important truth. That is, the only way that we can protect our citizens as individuals from having their lives and liberties snatched away by outside interference, is to prevent the same liberty and outside interference being inflicted on the very nation and Parliament who are supposed to protect and answer to them.

---

[141] ABC News, *'Germany allows comedian to face prosecution over satire of Turkish leader Recep Tayyip Erdogan'*, [15th April 2016], Retreived 28th April 2016 -
http://www.abc.net.au/news/2016-04-16/angela-merkel-criticised-for-allowing-prosecution-of-comedian/7331848

CHAPTER 14
HABEAS BRITANNIAM

After the journey we have taken, the question we should ask ourselves should be; what has the EU taken from us? The answer is 'everything'. The EU's idea of 'free trade' is actually a suppression of real competition that stifles small business and empowers corporations in obtaining monopolies. There is little use in denying the fact that TTIP will see our services, industries and worker's rights trampled under the foot. Additionally, we have witnessed how the EU penalises nations and criminalises individuals for daring to look after their own interests and failing to observe even the slightest orders. We have seen how the idea of 'Human Rights' is actually an impotent, unreliable falsity standing idly by in the face of political discrimination and genuine injustice. You have witnessed the imprisonment of innocent British citizens, the prosecution of German comedians, the hijacking of our own national achievements to be cheapened as propaganda for a failing pseudo-state, the overhauling of democracy and the threatening of the very values, institutions and principles that have protected us for centuries. Indeed, the EU has even cast aside our constitution and all of its achievements; the rule of law, habeas corpus, the right to fair trial by jury, and many more. We have seen, the very sovereignty of parliament drained away and replaced with an unaccountable lawmaking body akin to a regime we fought long ago. Ultimately, we have seen our nation handed over into enslavement; subjugated and devoid of real authority.

The reality is that the legal system, laws and governing bodies that dictate the rules by which you live your life, are perhaps the most important aspects of your worldly existence. So vital it is then, that you take note of what you have seen here, and move forward with a knew consciousness about your own self-worth, which can only be manifest in recognising the worth of the gifts that your nation has bestowed upon you.

Lord Denning once described the Magna Carta, perhaps our greatest achievement, as *"The greatest constitutional document of all times – the foundation of the freedom of the individual against the arbitrary authority of the despot*[142]*"* I hope, by now, that you can see that your individual freedoms rest on your autonomy and sovereignty. A man in a nation that is not free, is not free. So, when I say 'Habeas Britanniam', what I really mean is: may you say *"No"* to this deficient EU legal order, and instead, 'may you have Britain', and may Britain be free.

---

[142] Lee, Simon; *'Lord Denning, Magna Carta and Magnanimity';* Denning Law Journal, [Vol. 27 2015]

ABOUT THE AUTHOR

Dominic Bardill was born in Leicester on the 26th of September 1989. He grew up in Broughton Astley; a village in South Leicestershire. Dominic speaks French and received his legal education at BPP Law School, where he gained his LLB in Law. He intends to pursue his legal career further by studying the BPTC at the University of Law, where he has been awarded the 'Provosts Award for Excellence'. Dominic hopes to carve out a successful career as a 'Barrister-at-Law' in the future, so that he can dedicate his life to advocating for liberty and sovereignty; and practise law for his bread and butter.

www.ingramcontent.com/pod-product-compliance
Lightning Source LLC
Chambersburg PA
CBHW030942180526
45163CB00002B/672